BEYOND GREED

BRIAN ROSNER

PLUS BONUS CHAPTERS BY PHILLIP JENSEN, JOHN DICKSON, BROUGHTON KNOX, TONY PAYNE AND OTHERS

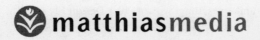

Beyond Greed
© Matthias Media, 2004

Matthias Media
(St Matthias Press Ltd. ACN 067 558 365)
PO Box 225
Kingsford NSW 2032 Australia
Telephone: (02) 9663 1478; Facsimile: (02) 9663 3265
International: +61-2-9663 1478; Facsimile +61-2-9663 3265
Email: info@matthiasmedia.com.au
Internet: www.matthiasmedia.com.au

Distributed in South Africa by:
Christian Book Discounters
Telephone: (021) 685 3663
Email: peter@christianbooks.co.za

Distributed in the United Kingdom by:
The Good Book Company
Telephone: 0845-225-0880
Facsimile: 0845-225-0990
Email: admin@thegoodbook.co.uk
Internet: www.thegoodbook.co.uk

ISBN 1 876326 76 X

Cover design and typesetting by Lankshear Design Pty Ltd.

Contents

Foreword . . . .*page 7*

Preface . . . .*page 9*

Preface to the second edition . . . .*page 13*

PART I: UNMASKING GREED

Chapter 1: The six deadly sins . . . .*page 17*

More to the matter . . . .*page 27*

Chasing fantasies . . . .*page 29*

Chapter 2 The prosperity gospel . . . .*page 33*

PART II: GREED IS IDOLATRY

Chapter 3: Secret idolatry . . . .*page 45*

Chapter 4: Inordinate love . . . .*page 55*

Chapter 5: Misplaced trust . . . .*page 67*

Chapter 6: Forbidden service . . . .*page 77*

PART III: LEARNING CONTENTMENT

Chapter 7: Contentment and the knowledge of God . .*page 89*

The secret of contentment . . . .*page 101*

This present age: our struggle not to covet . . . .*page 107*

PART IV: SHARING POSSESSIONS

Chapter 8: The significance of giving in the
early church . . . .*page 117*

How to have a financial meltdown . . . .*page 130*

Faith and works; rich and poor . . . .*page 135*

PART V: A CHRISTIAN LIFESTYLE

The Christian and money . . . .*page 146*

Not keeping up with the Joneses . . . .*page 152*

PART VI: TRUE RICHES

Chapter 9: True riches . . . .*page 163*

TO LIL, EM AND WILL

FOREWORD

THERE ARE MANY SIGNS in our society that greed has got out of hand. Incomes are double today what they were a generation ago, and technology has eased the burden of many routine tasks. So why do we need to work even harder, and for even longer hours? Is it really out of economic necessity, or simply to afford more toys for the children?

Why is there still such competition between political parties to reduce taxes, even when this leads to industry-crippling interest rates and loss of jobs? The result is that the rich just get richer and the poor poorer. And where will the government find the money to pay for essential improvements in education and health-care provision?

The Bible tells us to look after the poor, especially the 'fatherless and widows'. Our cities are now full of fatherless teenagers and abandoned wives. And we, in our greed, have abandoned them too.

Then there's the time-bomb of pensions. A generation which puts off having children because they spoil its enjoyment of the good things of life is going against the wisdom of the ages. We need children to look after us when we can no longer look after ourselves. The falling birth rate has created a huge gap in the income needed to provide the pensions of this high-spending generation.

No government, of any political persuasion, can afford to ignore the opinion of voters. If Brian Rosner's well-reasoned appeal to the conscience can influence individuals, it may succeed in making an impact on government policies which promote greed.

The sin of covetousness, laid bare by this excellent book, shows that Christians must be part of the counter-culture, resistant to the TV ads and to the skewed priorities of our consumer culture. Giving is the antidote to selfishness, but is also a command for Christians. If we take that command seriously, maybe the world will take us seriously.

Sir Fred Catherwood

PREFACE

THIS BOOK CONSISTS OF Christian reflections on greed, contentment and giving in the modern world. Needless to say, the original title, *How to Be Really Rich*, was thought preferable to this rather dull, if accurate, description of the book's contents. It is not a balanced and irenic survey of the Bible's teaching on possessions.[1] Nor is it a book of practical advice on how we should deal with our money. It would be less than honest, however, to say that I am not interested in changing behaviour, both mine and yours. The book is an attempt to disturb our pockets, not with practical tips and specific appeals, but rather by warming our hearts and clearing our heads. I am convinced that such change best comes about by changing the way we think about ourselves, the world and God. This is the strategy Paul recommends in Romans 12:2: "... be transformed by the renewal of your mind".

Our look at greed is 'sharp' in the sense of forceful and satirical, in that when reflecting on the teaching relevant to our topic in the Bible, the dominant notes struck are those of irony and ridicule. Money is one of those areas where the Bible stands against us and offers us an alternative vision. The satire, however, stops short of outright scorn, since I make no claim to being anything but complicit in the follies the book attempts to expose. On the contrary, if the book affords any insight, it is usually due to first-hand experience of the sins it condemns. Whether the book is sharp in the sense of incisive is for the reader to decide.

Following the Bible's lead, greed is analysed as a *religion*,

9

as nothing less than a sophisticated form of idolatry. The book sets out to deliver both a challenge and comfort to people who feel dissatisfied with the materialism of our age.

Greed has been glamorized, and is a forgotten sin. A major goal of this book is to reveal its true hideousness, and to restore its hard-won, well-deserved reputation. Although greed can be profitably analysed in terms of sociological, psychological and economic factors, its root cause can be understood only with the help of theology. Greed is a theological problem. To leave the question of God out of our attempts to understand greed is to treat the problem superficially. Whether or not the reader is a Christian, my goal is to show that God offers in his word, the Bible, not only a penetrating diagnosis of greed, but also, and more importantly, the ultimate cure for greed.

Writing a book against greed could be said to be doomed to failure from the start. "Deploring money and its effects is a treasured occupation for those people who like to feel virtuous", writes psychologist Dorothy Rowe. "Doing so is as useful as deploring the fact that we need air to breathe".[2] Indeed, many have observed that greed (of one sort or another) is inevitable for the human species. Rowe puts the matter simply: "I think that the only way to give up being greedy is to die".[3] The philosopher Immanuel Kant likewise observed that "insatiability belongs to the basic makeup of human beings".[4] And the theologian Eberhard Jüngel concurs: "Striving for more is human".[5]

Thus in one sense the only hope in the fight against greed is not to fight those insatiable urges for more, but to redirect them. This, as we shall see, is what the Bible recommends. There is nothing wrong with wanting to get really rich, as long as riches are properly defined.

In 1996–7 I spent a sabbatical at the University of Tübingen in Germany as a Humboldt Fellow doing research for an academic monograph on the subject of greed and idolatry in the ancient world. The obvious relevance of this material to the modern world slowly dawned on me, at which point the idea for this book was conceived. A number of people have helped in various ways with its delivery. Thanks are due to Anke and Matthias Kumpf, Sheana and Peter Brown, Tracy and Graham Robertson, Kevin Reid, Alan Storkey, Audrey Dawson, my parents, and IVP editor Stephanie Heald. I am particularly grateful to Richard Firmin for giving me the final push to finish. The book is dedicated to three of my treasures, the priceless Elizabeth and Emily and that wee gem William.

ENDNOTES
1. For this, see Craig Blomberg, *Neither Poverty nor Riches: A Biblical Theology of Possessions* (Leicester: Apollos, 1999).
2. Dorothy Rowe, *The Real Meaning of Money* (London: HarperCollins, 1997), p. ix.
3. Rowe, *The Real Meaning of Money*, p. 184.
4. Cited in Miroslav Volf, 'In the Cage of Vanities: Christian Faith and the Dynamics of Economic Progress', in Robert Wuthnow (ed.), *Rethinking Materialism: Perspectives on the Spiritual Dimension of Economic Behaviour* (Grand Rapids: Eerdmans, 1995), p. 172.
5. Jüngel, 'Gewinn in Himmel und auf Erden: Theologische Bemerkungen zum Streben und Gewinn', *Zeitschrift für Theologie und Kirche* 94.4 (1997), p. 547.

PREFACE TO THE SECOND EDITION

THIS BOOK WAS ORIGINALLY, in effect, an exposition of two short biblical texts: Colossians 3:5, "Greed ... is idolatry", and 1 Timothy 6:6, "There is great gain in godliness with contentment".

The second edition includes all of the original text, but has been expanded in several ways. In each section, articles from *The Briefing* have been selected which reflect further upon the issues raised in my text, and give very practical advice about putting the principles we learn into practice.[*]
I have also written a new chapter, 'The prosperity gospel', which is in Section I.

[*] For more information about *The Briefing*, see page 176.

Greed ... is idolatry.
COLOSSIANS 3:5

There is great gain in godliness with contentment.
1 TIMOTHY 6:6

*For what will it profit a man if he gains
the whole world and forfeits his life?*
MATTHEW 16:26

I

UNMASKING GREED

CHAPTER 1

THE SIX DEADLY SINS

NOTHING BEATS THE exhilaration of trading on the floor at a major stock exchange, so I'm told. All of us have seen pictures of the frenzied buying and selling in which a fortune can be won or lost depending on whether the deal is made at precisely the right moment. Three of the slogans on Wall Street sum up the sentiments of most of those involved: "Buy or die" and "Lunch is for wimps" proclaim the urgency of the activity; and "Greed is good" captures its driving motivation.

Most of us would stop short of affirming that greed is good. That is to state the matter rather too strongly. We have a more nuanced attitude towards money. If asked what is more important to us, we would not hesitate to put family and friends ahead of material things. We are also quite prepared to condemn the massive pay rises which company directors grant themselves as nothing less than obscene. And we shake our heads in disgust at the wanton acquisitiveness of Imelda Marcos, whose collection of shoes outnumbered most people's stamp collections, or at the self-destructive avarice of Nick Leeson, whose lust for money brought down Barings Bank.

Yet our attitude to money can be quite contradictory. Although, when speaking generally about the human condition, we say that everyone loves money, we are usually not willing to say the same in reference to ourselves.

Money is in fact the last great social taboo. Whereas once

it was thought rude or at least tactless to speak about sex or politics in polite conversation, these days it seems that only the subject of money is unmentionable. In most Western societies at least, one is not permitted to ask individuals how much they earn or what they do with their money. When it comes to money, most of us are very secretive.

Why is this the case? Dorothy Rowe puts it down to shame, humiliation and envy.[1] Money is a measure of success. There is shame in being hard up and pride in being well-heeled. An amusing example concerns the unfavourable publicity the British Chancellor of the Exchequer received when it was disclosed that the limit on his credit card was surprisingly low. For many people, to know someone else's net worth would evoke one of two responses: either envy or disdain. Money is the simplest measure of whether you are winning at the game of life.

Most people, it is true, would not say that greed is good. If the phenomenon of national lotteries is anything to go by, however, the vast majority of us are rather keen on the idea of getting really rich. Christians are, it seems, no different. A survey of regular churchgoers in the USA found that almost 90% say greed is a sin; fewer than 20% say they were ever taught that wanting a lot of money is wrong, and almost 80% say that they wish they had more money than they do.[2]

Insatiability is of course not unique to modern Western civilization. Greed has always been with us. As Miroslav Volf has observed, however, "cultural acceptance, even encouragement, of insatiability is unique to modernity ... The inactive virus of insatiability broke out with capitalism in a general epidemic".[3] It is probably fair to say that even though greed remains a vice in most people's minds, it has been devalued.

One preacher suggested four reasons why Christians do

not often hold greed to be as grave as, for instance, sexual immorality:

> *Because, (1) it is so common; (2) because it is found among those who make pretensions to refinement and even religion; (3) because it is not so easy to define what is covetousness, as it is to define impurity of life; and (4) because the public conscience is seared, and the mind blinded to the low and grovelling character of the sin.*[4]

Greed today is, by comparison with times past, a trivial sin. 'Don't be greedy' is most commonly heard when someone wants a second piece of chocolate cake. Greed may even be said to be a public good, the engine which drives economic progress. The condemnation of greed is the last thing in the mind of the media when interviewing or reporting a story about some fabulously wealthy celebrity. And even though, if you stop to think about it, greed makes many people's lives a misery, modern psychology generally does not take greed to be a problem worth treating. Try asking the relatives of a workaholic or a compulsive gambler if they agree. A retired priest recounted that in his long years of service all kinds of sins and concerns were confessed to him in the confessional, but never once the sin of greed.

In politics, and even in music and sport, 'the bottom line' is apparently all that counts these days. Political campaigns are regularly fought by appealing without shame or qualms to the greed of voters. Which party is promising the biggest tax cut? Other values are swept aside compared to the party's ability to manage the economy to the end of enriching its citizens. Ex-Beatle George Harrison once lamented the modern recording industry's raw commercialism: "Whatever you play, the most important thing is to sell and make money. It's got nothing to do with talent".[5] Vexatious litigation is frequently what follows success; as one manager put it: "Where there's a hit, there's a writ". One football fan made a similar observation about a report concerning his team, Manchester United plc, which dwelt on a £44 million turnover and an £11 million profit, and mentioned only in passing their winning the Premier League and the FA Cup: "Manchester United, with its great history and inspiring legends, has grown cynical and arrogant in its mad pursuit of money ... Bigger salaries have made players and managers just as greedy as the clubs".[6]

Greed is almost an Olympic sport, if the behaviour of certain members of the International Olympic Committee is anything to go by. A select band of its members apparently received money, jewellery, free medical care and educational scholarships in exchange for their votes concerning the destination of the 2002 Olympic flame. The traditional slogan, 'Faster, higher, stronger', has been adapted, as one newspaper editorial put it, to 'Cash, cheques, credit cards'. Those who offered the 'incentives' to the IOC members saw no cause for blushing, claiming in their defence that they had simply been following a long-established (if not terribly honourable) Olympic tradition.

How many tales of woe could be told which involve the destruction of families over the matter of the Will? As someone once said, where there is a Will, there is a war. Many a wealthy family has been torn apart over the inheritance that a child had expected and didn't get. Apparently, the bigger the cake, the more we fight over our share. That money is a cause of domestic strife in families which are not well off also goes without saying. In such cases the lack of money can of course be a genuine factor, but more often than not one party will be quick to accuse the other of acting out of greed.

Greed is often the motivation behind a whole range of other more obviously destructive behaviours. In the USA there was a rise in professional murders from fewer than 1,000 in 1980 to over 5,000 in 1997. The FBI puts this down to tougher divorce laws, which force the guilty party to fork out more money. Apparently, if the figures add up, aggrieved spouses hire assassins to kill their partners. One agent, who regularly poses as a hit-man in order to apprehend the culprits, explains their motives:

> They're basically driven by greed and jealousy. The clients are treating somebody's life as just an annoying obstacle to what they want ... People think: they want my money. They deserve to die.[7]

It is diffcult to comprehend the fact that the greed of one person can have an adverse effect on the lives of tens of millions of people. Nevertheless it is true. Indonesia's economic problems in the late 1990s, which led to widespread poverty and the eruption of numerous riots, doubtless have complex causes; the blame cannot be easily apportioned. The fact that President Suharto's personal wealth has been estimated at $16 billion and that of his family at $40 billion, however, cannot be overlooked. It is a cruel coincidence that the International Monetary Fund's rescue plan for the country's ailing economy came to about the same figure.[8] The long-running joke in Indonesia is that so pervasive is the Suharto family's reach into the economy that they start profiting from your visit as soon as you arrive at the airport in Jakarta: if you buy a packet of cigarettes, take a taxi, pay the toll on the road into the city, check into a hotel, and so on, with each step money goes into the family's pockets.

Greedy behaviour is taken for granted, as can be seen from the way we respond to the exceptions. Aaron Feuerstein owned a textile mill in Massachusetts. Two weeks before Christmas the plant was burned to the ground. Everyone assumed that he would take the insurance money and run, to the financial detriment of the employees. After all, what else would a businessman with any sense do? Instead, Feuerstein told his staff that they would be kept on full pay over the holiday period and given a Christmas bonus. In other words, he did the decent thing. Apparently, decency is abnormal. President Clinton invited Mr Feuerstein to his State of the Union address and there proclaimed him an American hero.[9]

It would in fact be hard to understand the modern world without some reference to greed. The second half of the twentieth century was dominated by the Cold War and the rise and fall of communism. It is pure irony that the system which set itself against the greed of capitalism, was eventually brought down in part by the greed of its own governing classes.

You could say that there are three major current threats to our existence as individuals and societies: pollution, terrorism and crime. In each case greed can take a good share of the credit. Pollution is caused and continues to be caused by human unwillingness to pay the price for the cleaner alternatives. We don't lack the technology, just the will. On any reckoning, climatic change due to the effects of pollution could cause major 'natural' disasters in the days to come. In most cases of terrorism, each side accuses the other of some form of greed, whether involving people, land or property. Greed also fits both sides of the equation in many cases of crime. Thieves steal because they want more and often because they perceive the victims as having more than their fair share.

Christian attitudes to greed

Christians have not always regarded greed so lightly. In fact, according to the New Testament, greed qualifies as one of the most serious of sins. The earliest Christians were told not just to avoid greed, but to watch out for it (Luke 12:15), to flee from it (1 Tim 6:10–11) or to kill it (Col 3:5). Greed is described in most unflattering terms. It is "a root of all kinds of evils" (1 Tim 6:10), one of the twelve things which come out of individuals and defile them (Mark 7:20–22), and evidence of a darkened understanding or a depraved mind (Eph 4:18–19; Rom 1:28–29). Worst of all, greed is said to be a form of idolatry. Jesus went as far as to tell a parable which is directed specifically against greed, in which God chastises the protagonist with the word, "Fool!" (Luke 12:16–20). Furthermore, greed is thought to lead to other sins, including theft, pride and sexual immorality.

Indeed, there is a wealth of evidence from the Old Testament and early Jewish moral teaching which supports a link between greed and injustice. Most of the hostility to wealth which can be found in the Old Testament is linked to the failure of the rich to act justly towards the stranger, the widow, the orphan and the poor. The wealthy man is equated with the wicked (Ps 10:3), the violent (Prov 11:16) and the proud (Prov 15:25, 16:19; Isa 2:7, 11, 13:11; Jer 51:13). The rich are those who "carry out evil devices" (Ps 37:7) and offer bribes (Prov 17:8). Furthermore, wealth is often linked with wickedness (Prov 10:2, 11:28; 22:1, cf. Ps 37:16; Prov 15:16, 16:8, 17:1, 28:6). The first ethical concern to be mentioned in Proverbs is the band of outlaws whose goal it is to "find all precious goods" and to "fill [their] houses with plunder" (1:13); wisdom warns that such people "run to evil" and "make haste to shed blood" (1:16). In Proverbs 19:22 it is taken for granted that the greedy are liars. In Micah 2:2, "They covet fields and seize them".

Similarly, Philo observes that "injustice is bred by anxious thought for the means of life and for money-making".[10] Riches and injustice are associated in one of the Dead Sea Scrolls: "men of injustice ... who are zealous after wealth".[11] And an early Jewish rabbinic commentary states that "if you desire you will covet; and if you covet you will tyrannize and rob".[12]

In Revelation 18, where the fall of Babylon is announced, her sumptuous wealth and extravagance are tainted when the merchants' list of cargo, which opens with "gold, silver, jewels, pearls", closes emphatically with "slaves, that is, human souls" (vv. 12–13), suggesting that the city's prosperity and luxury rely on brutality and contempt for human life. This impression is confirmed in 18:21, where Babylon is condemned as a blood-shedding city of violence, produced and maintained by military force. Babylon epitomizes the ruthlessness of greed.

If you were to ask the apostle Paul or someone else in the early church to construct a profile of your average pagan, someone who does not know the true and living God, you would probably have got a three-point sermon in response. Early Jews and Christians alike condemned the Gentiles first of all for their idolatry, then for their sexual immorality and finally for their greed. In Luke 12:22–30, for example, the Gentiles are described as those whose lifestyle is characterized by a relentless seeking after material things. In the letter of Polycarp, written soon after the close of the New Testament, greed is specifically distinguished as being a mark of the heathen (11:2).

On only two occasions in Acts is the opposition to the early church specifically non-Jewish. In both cases financial considerations caused the problems. When Paul, in Philippi, cast the demon of divination out of the slave girl (16:16–18), her owners, who were incensed over their loss of income (v. 19), brought him before the magistrates to be flogged and imprisoned (vv. 20–24). Later, Paul's stand against idolatry led to a riot instigated by the silversmiths, who made the shrines to the goddess Artemis and regarded the apostle as a threat to their livelihood (19:23–41).

To put the matter the other way around, greed not only suits a pagan's lifestyle, it is also not a fitting behaviour for someone who knows God. In Colossians 3, Paul encourages the church not to be greedy because such behaviour is incompatible with a genuinely Christian lifestyle. Likewise, according to 1 Corinthians 5:11, people who claim to be Christians and are nevertheless greedy do not belong in the church and should be excluded.

Christendom before the modern period took greed just as seriously. In the fourth century, Zeno of Verona declared simply: "God is right to hate greed".[13] The greedy are as insatiable as hell, according to Basil the Great: "Hell never says enough is enough; neither does greed ever say enough".[14] Ambrose thought greed so central that he spoke of the primal sin, that of Adam in the garden, not as original sin, but as 'original greed'.

In the Middle Ages, an important vehicle for moral teaching was the list of so-called seven deadly sins: pride, lust, gluttony, sloth, anger, envy and greed. Although Gregory the Great placed pride ahead of greed at the top of the list, in the numerous expositions in the centuries following him greed usually took pride of place. Medical metaphors were often used to describe the effects greed can have on people. Greed was not only a deadly sin, but a deadly disease. Greed was commonly thought to be the spiritual equivalent of dropsy, which involves an insatiable thirst for water even though the body is already filled with fluid. The more the addicted person tries to satisfy the thirst, the more it is stimulated. So it was thought to be the case with greed.[15]

In the Protestant Reformation, greed maintained its bad reputation. According to Martin Luther, for instance, greed causes unbelief, and unbelief causes greed. Luther took the fourth request of the Lord's prayer, "Give us today our daily bread", as a call to shun greed. He also urged every Christian to undertake regular and earnest prayer against this dangerous vice.

Over the ages, greed has been recognized for what it is— destructive, deceitful and contrary to God. It is truly a deadly sin. Yet it is the sin we have forgotton.

ENDNOTES

1. Dorothy Rowe, *The Real Meaning of Money*, pp. 148-151.
2. Reported in Robert Wuthnow, *God and Mammon in America* (New York: The Free Press, 1994), p. 126.
3. Miroslav Volf, 'In the Cage of Vanities: Christian Faith and the Dynamics of Economic Progress', p. 172.
4. Albert Barnes, *Notes Explanatory and Practical on the Epistles of Paul* (New York: Harper Brothers, 1845), p. 317.
5. George Harrison in *The Times*, 28 August 1995, p. 5.
6. Reported in Rowe, *The Real Meaning of Money*, p. 206.
7. *The Times Magazine*, 15 August 1998, p. 36.
8. *The Times*, 18 March 1998, p. 25.
9. *The Guardian*, 25 March 1996.
10. Philo, *On the Contemplative Life* 17.
11. 1QS 11:1-2.
12. *Mekilta* Exodus 20:17.
13. Zeno of Verona, *On Greed* 1.11.
14. Basil the Great, *Sermon to the Rich* 5.
15. Solomon Schimmel, *The Seven Deadly Sins* (New York: The Free Press, 1992), p. 18.

MORE TO THE MATTER
Carmelina Read[*]

A FEW YEARS AGO I went to the funeral of a lady I worked with. She was in her late 30s and had two small children. This lady was a workaholic. She used to regularly work until the early hours of the morning. Even after she got a fever from stress and overwork, she kept on working. Eventually her sickness got worse. She got pneumonia. She was rushed to hospital. And a few days later she died. At her funeral, her husband spoke. He said that his little girl had asked him where Mummy was now. And I'll never forget what he told her.

He said, "Mummy doesn't exist any more".

It was the best summary of materialism I had heard in a long while.

There's nothing beyond this life. There's no spiritual realm. Matter is all that matters. That was their philosophy. And if you think about it, this couple lived what they believed. They worked for everything this life could offer them. From a materialist perspective they had everything: nice house, cars, kids, holidays, prestigious careers. Their philosophy led to a lifestyle of materialism. They believed in materialism. And that's how they lived.

I know that's an extreme example, but it is how most people live. The great Australian dream is by-and-large a materialistic dream. Even if they don't fully believe it, most people *live* as if matter is all that matters. Sadly, too many Christians also fit the description.

Jesus spoke some words which directly oppose the materialistic view of life. Before telling the parable of the Rich Fool, Jesus said, "One's life does not consist in the abundance of his possessions". Jesus radically opposes the idea that our lives are all about what we *have*: that what we can see, hear, smell, taste and touch is ultimate reality. Jesus says that life is *not* just made up of material things.

* Originally published in *The Briefing*, #279.

There's more to it. Our life is something *separate* from what we have. There's a reality beyond what we can see, hear, smell, touch and taste.

Jesus teaches that those who view life materialistically are just wrong. Therefore, greed—the constant striving to get things—is a wrong response to reality. It's a foolish way to live. It might make sense if materialism were true. But it isn't. A man's life does not consist in the abundance of his possessions.

If a non-Christian were to describe your life, what would they say? Can they see any difference between you and your non-Christian neighbour? The fact is, for the most part you can't see any difference between Christians and non-Christians in terms of the way we deal with our possessions. We say we believe in Jesus. We say matter isn't all that matters. But at the same time we own just as much as our neighbours. And we spend just as much time worrying about our possessions as our neighbours do. We've got the same dreams, the same goals as our non-Christian neighbours. We still spend the majority of our time working for a successful career. Like our pagan neighbours, we spend most of our money on our houses, our cars, our kids' education, our holidays, our overseas trips, our superannuation and retirement funds, investments, nice clothes and furniture. It's just that we baptize it and call it Christian stewardship.

The other day in Bible study, a friend of mine asked for prayer. She explained that she and her husband are looking for a house to buy. I thought she might be asking for prayer about which house to buy or where. But instead she said something very surprising and very honest. She said she realized that she was spending a lot of her time worrying about buying a house. Every day she stewed about it. It was all she could think about. She wanted us to pray that God would help her to stop worrying and to concentrate instead on serving him. On being a good wife and mother. On helping those in her church. She wanted prayer that she'd keep house hunting in perspective. And I guess that's the key. We need to keep all these material things in perspective: our lives do not consist in the abundance of them.

CHASING FANTASIES
Andrew Lansdown[*]

WHEN I THINK ABOUT gambling I think about a comment our first daughter made when she was just six years old. Overhearing my wife and I discussing whether or not we had enough money to buy something, she chipped in, "Why don't you buy a Lotto ticket? Then you'll get some money."

Of course, our daughter had seen advertisements on television claiming that the way to get rich was through the lotteries. She had also seen lottery tickets clipped to a Christian friend's fridge. And I suppose she had heard talk of Lotto at school. So I should not have been surprised at her remark. But I was. Indeed, it set me thinking about the social and moral impact of gambling, even 'lowkey' gambling like the lotteries.

I have always opposed gambling for four reasons.

Firstly, gambling undermines frugal living. It wastes money. Few gamblers ever make a profit. Most, over a lifetime and proportionate to their incomes, make enormous losses. Better to throw a dollar in the gutter than to place it on a bet. At least that way you will not be troubled and thrilled by the prospect of it turning into a million dollars and thereby be tempted to throw another dollar after it.

Secondly, gambling undermines self-control. It is addictive. It creates a craving for more gambling. Through my work as an education officer in Western Australian prisons I met men who had lost their possessions, professions, families and freedom through compulsive gambling.

Thirdly, gambling undermines social justice. It produces misery and inequity. Through gambling, people are impoverished and families shattered. Lives are utterly ruined. And the community at large is burdened with the cost of keeping men in prison

[*] Originally published in *The Briefing*, #263.

and families on pensions.

Fourthly, gambling undermines virtuous character. It promotes selfishness and greed. It arises from and gives rise to a love of money. It corrupts people's affections, focusing them on the getting of wealth and material things.

However, after hearing my daughter's remarks, I realized there is another reason to oppose gambling. And I think that this reason is the most compelling of all:

Fifthly, gambling undermines right perceptions. It distorts reality. It supplants financial certainties with financial fantasies. It perverts people's understandings of how to 'get ahead'. It leads them to believe that Lotto is the means by which they can meet their needs and make their fortunes. In short, it blinds people to the right way to get money.

Honest work and careful stewardship are the primary ways that God has ordained for people to satisfy their material needs and wants. Concerning the importance of work, Solomon states, "A slack hand causes poverty, but the hand of the diligent makes rich" (Prov 10:4). Concerning the importance of saving and investing, Solomon states, "Precious treasure and oil are in a wise man's dwelling, but a foolish man devours it" (Prov 21:20).

Earn money with diligence, spend it with prudence: this is the path to prosperity that God affirms and that gambling denies. And no form of gambling denies it more effectively than the lotteries.

Every week of the year, hundreds of thousands of people who do not otherwise gamble, wager tens of millions of dollars on lottery tickets. Along with their money, they waste their time and hopes. Their lives are on constant hold as they fantasize over the question, "What you gonna do when you win Lotto?"

A friend once told me that she and her husband wanted to buy a new car. She explained how they had searched in vain for an affordable vehicle, and concluded our conversation by saying, "Anyway, we're hoping to win the lotteries soon, then we'll be able to buy one".

Around the same time, a neighbour came (as was his habit) to borrow my car trailer. As he hooked it up he said, "This might be the last time I have to borrow it. I'm gonna win Lotto soon; then I'll get my own trailer."

Both my friend and my neighbour were quite serious. They saw the lotteries as the answer to their financial difficulties and dreams. They were not saving for the things they wanted. Rather, they were using the money that could have been saved to buy lottery tickets. They were bewitched by fantasies of the Lotto life.

Christians would be wise to resist the lure of lotteries, and of all other forms of gambling. We should practise and promote God's means of meeting material needs and getting material wealth. We should work hard and save well—and teach our children to do the same. For the basic financial principles expressed by God through Solomon in Proverbs 28:19 still hold: "Whoever works his land will have plenty of bread, but he who follows worthless pursuits will have plenty of poverty".

CHAPTER 2

THE PROSPERITY GOSPEL

THE FAMILIAR ADAGE, 'let the buyer beware', is no longer true. These days suppliers are obliged to make accurate statements about their products. You can read on the label exactly what's in the box, down to the last component, constituent element or crumb (e.g. 'may contain traces of peanuts'), and what it can do to or for you (e.g. 'tranquiliser: may cause drowsiness')—false or unrealistic claims are against the law. Unfortunately, there are no trading standards for the Christian faith, and many times those who commend the gospel make claims about its blessings which do not stand up to scrutiny. What are the 'money-back' guarantees of the gospel? What can each and every one of us who trust in Jesus expect as a result?

A recent and growing phenomenon in popular Christian teaching is what may be called the prosperity gospel. Not a few preachers in the Western world encourage people to become Christians because of the material benefits that will surely follow. Brian Houston, of the Hills Christian Life Centre in Sydney, is one example. In what follows I respond to his book, *You Need More Money: Discovering God's Amazing Financial Plan for Your Life* (Castle Hill: Maximised Leadership, 1999). My comments are not a general or personal judgment; I merely respond to his ideas.

In *You Need More Money*, Houston claims that "the scriptures ... [are] full of promises of prosperity" (p. 10). He summarizes the goal of the book as follows:

> *If you and I can change our thinking and develop a*
> *healthy attitude towards money, I believe we can all walk*
> *in the blessing and prosperity that God intends for us.*
> *We will never have a problem with money again* (P. 3).

Not unrelated is his exhortation that "[I]f you are struggling with your health, know that it is the will of God to see you whole and healthy. Health is one of the promises of God for our lives" (p. 31). A number of American televangelists make similar claims, with book titles like, *Redeemed from Poverty and Sickness* and *God's Will is Prosperity*. Few salesmen would pass up the chance to sell a product that promises nothing less than health and wealth!

What are we to make of such teaching? Before taking a brief look at *You Need More Money*, it is helpful to consider a section of Paul's letter to the Romans where he lists what he considers to be the biggest boons of being a Christian.

The benefits of peace with God

In Romans 5:1-11, Paul's mood changes from cool and collected to rapturous ecstasy. Up until this point in the letter, he has been occupied laying a charge against the entire human race (all are under sin's power and condemnation) and announcing what God has done through Christ to remedy the situation (justification by grace through faith). In chapters 1-4, almost everything is in the third person and in the past tense: Christ did this, God did that, Abraham believed, and so on. But in chapter five he switches gear, moving to the first person and the present tense: we have this, we have that. His exuberance is unmissable as he bounces from idea to idea. Make no mistake, Paul is no less enthusiastic about the benefits of peace with God than the most flamboyant prosperity preacher.

Such is Paul's excitement, that the argument of the paragraph is not easy to trace. It doesn't have the tight logical structure of the previous sections. One clue to grasping his message is to notice the three-fold repetition of the verb "to rejoice", the first two of which appear in verses two and three:

> *Therefore, since we have been justified by faith, we have peace with God through our Lord Jesus Christ. Through him we have also obtained access by faith into this grace in which we stand, and we rejoice in hope of the glory of God. More than that, we rejoice in our sufferings, knowing that suffering produces endurance, and endurance produces character, and character produces hope, and hope does not put us to shame, because God's love has been poured into our hearts through the Holy Spirit who has been given to us* (5:1-5).

Rather than guaranteeing health and wealth, Paul's gospel, it seems, brings something very different, namely hope and hardship. The surprising thing is that Paul thinks this is good news, something worth boasting about, as much as someone might show off their new house or car. The verb "to rejoice" (5:2-3) is in fact the same word as in 3:27, where most Bible versions translate it "boast": "Then what becomes of our boasting? It is excluded". Paul rules out, in chapter 3, boasting of the 'what I've got or done' variety, only to replace it in chapter 5 with boasting about what God has done "through our Lord Jesus Christ".

Paul thinks we can boast about our hope and sufferings. Let's consider them in turn. First, peace with God guarantees *glory in the future.* Christian hope for Paul is not baseless optimism (like the young girl *hopes* to travel to Mars, or *hopes* to marry Prince William). Like our notion of hope, biblical hope is full of strong desire, but the difference is for Paul that this longing is combined with a certain expectation. As the NIV puts it, "hope does not disappoint" (5:5a). Christians have an absolute assurance of a glorious future with God beyond the grave. Understandably, this hope gives us great pleasure in the mere anticipation of that day, as we relish the thought.

Admittedly, knowing that peace with God guarantees *sufferings in the present* sounds less agreeable. To avoid misunderstanding, it is worth noting that the early Christians were not masochistic nor anti-pleasure; asceticism arose among some Christians in the second century from Greek rather than biblical roots. Rather, Paul says there are three reasons to rejoice in our troubles.

Firstly, we boast in suffering because of the beneficial results it produces. We rejoice because we know suffering yields endurance, which then shows our true character as God's children. The suffering Christian is like a new electronic circuit board in a "burn in environment" with a "full load" being tested, not so much to see whether, but to prove that all of its components will persevere. Similarly, God allows his children to suffer, not in order to break them, but to demonstrate their tried worth. To use New Testament metaphors, God the father disciplines his children, God the metal worker refines the gold in the fire and God the gardener prunes the vine. All three images point to an essential but painful process which is for our good. In short, troubles are good because they give us a fresh sense of our need for God and call us to depend on him.

Secondly, we boast in sufferings because of the hope it

engenders. Hope is both necessary for handling hardship and is strengthened by hardship. Like a cramped long-haul flight with plastic food and bad movies, calling to mind your destination makes it possible to endure present suffering. "For this slight momentary affliction is preparing for us an eternal weight of glory beyond all comparison" (2 Cor 4:17). Suffering in the present makes you look forward to a better future.

The third thing that makes it possible to boast in our hardship is the love of God. We see in verses 5-9 that what underlies Paul's positive thoughts about suffering is his firm conviction that God loves us: "God's love has been poured into our hearts ... God shows his love for us in that while we were still sinners, Christ died for us" (Rom 5:5, 8). God's love assures us that our negative experiences are not evidence that he is angry with us, for he knows us and our circumstances perfectly and has our welfare at heart. In the language of Romans 5:2, we "stand in grace", forgiven and adopted into his family. The suffering child of God is like the infant who stubs their toe and needs a reassuring cuddle from mum or dad as much as a bandaid.

Verse 11 supplies the third occurrence of rejoicing or boasting in Romans 5, which helps explain the first two: "More than that, *we also rejoice in God* through our Lord Jesus Christ". The reason hope and hardship are cause for elation is that they lead us to the great and gracious God, in whose right hand are pleasures forever.

Notice, though, that the two benefits Paul highlights as God's will for every Christian are a far cry from health and wealth. The contrast could hardly be more stark. The first relates to the future, and the second is the very opposite of the ease and comfort we associate with affluence. If this is the case, how then do some preachers advocate a prosperity gospel as opposed to a gospel of hardship and hope? The answer is that they misread the Bible.

A flat reading of Scripture

You Need More Money includes many exhortations to generous giving to God's work, and appropriate warnings "always to give God the glory for what he is doing in your life, especially in the area of blessing" (p. 103). It also offers lots of practical advice and what might be termed popular psychology (e.g. "If your self-esteem is low, you will never see yourself as valuable or worthwhile, and nor will anyone else", pp. 127-28). Our concern, however, is with its main theme, which Houston puts in the form of a question and answer: "Is it God's will for you to prosper? The answer is undoubtedly YES" (p. 55; capitals original).

This assertion is backed up with texts from across the Bible. The problem with Brian Houston's argument is that, when it comes to interpreting the Bible, he doesn't take into account the biblical context of those texts, and he also seems to have difficulty distinguishing between literal and metaphorical language. We will concentrate on a few key texts around which Houston builds his case.

Most of his proof texts come from the Old Testament and are read as if addressed directly to individual believers in Christ. Two of his favourites are Joshua 1:8 (pp. 20, 58) and Deuteronomy 8:17-18 (pp. 56, 95, 103). In the former text, Joshua is promised that if he meditates on the Law, "then you will make your way prosperous, and then you will have good success". Houston surmises that "prosperity is definitely a result of applying God's word to your life", and then asserts that "this is a specific promise from God and yet there are so many who don't believe it" (p. 20). "He [i.e. God] gives us the power and ability to get wealth through the principles and instructions of His word" (p. 58).

In context, however, the success and resultant prosperity promised to Joshua is as a commander of Israel's army as he seeks to "cause this people to inherit the land that I [i.e. God] swore to their fathers to give them" (1:6). The primary blessing under the old covenant was rest in the abundance of the land of milk and honey. Under the new covenant this rest is in the superabundance of heaven (Heb 4:1-11). Joshua 1:8 remains a valuable text calling for courage and fidelity to God's word, but its specific promise of material prosperity does not apply to Christians.

Deuteronomy 8:17-18 is similarly misunderstood. The text states: "You shall remember the LORD your God, for it is he who gives you power to get wealth" (v. 18). Houston comments: "[I]f you still aren't sure that God wants you to prosper, ask yourself ... why would He promise prosperity and success if He preferred us to remain poor?" (p. 56). However, the next sentence supplies the context of Moses' words: God blesses you thus "that he may confirm his covenant that he swore to your fathers". We no longer live under the law of Moses in the promised land. Put simply, for Christians such promises of prosperity are out of date, for Christ is the end of the law. Even in Old Testament times they were not understood absolutely, for as various Old Testament texts such as Job demonstrate, there was never a perfect correlation between righteous living and material blessing. Houston reads the Bible like a wide open plain, when it is actually more like a range of mountains. In other words, he fails to take into account the basic distinctions of salvation history that prevent serious misuse of Scripture.

A second problem concerns metaphorical language. A key text for Houston is 2 Corinthians 8:9, where Paul recalls the cost and purpose of the incarnation for the Son of God: "For you know the grace of our Lord Jesus Christ, that though he was rich, yet for your sake he became poor, so that you by his poverty might become rich". Houston's comments are worth quoting in full:

> I've heard people misinterpret this scripture to support their belief that it is biblical to be poor. They only read half of it, that "though He was rich, yet for your sakes He became poor". They completely miss the crucial point because if you read on, the reason why He became poor was that "you, through his poverty, might become rich". That is what it says. He became poor so YOU could become rich. The purpose of Jesus coming to earth included giving up a place of abundance and riches and becoming poor so that we could escape that poverty (PP. 12-13; EMPHASIS AND CAPITALS ORIGINAL).

Houston is right to declare that Jesus became poor so that we might become rich, but does not seem to realise that "rich" here is not meant to be taken literally. Instructively, the letter to the Laodiceans in Revelation has both the literal and metaphorical senses of riches in neighbouring verses. Jesus tells the literally rich they are spiritually poor, and need to become spiritually (or really) rich:

> For you say, I am (materially) rich, I have prospered, and I need nothing, not realizing that you are wretched, pitiable, (really) poor, blind, and naked. I counsel you to buy from me gold refined by fire, so that you may be (really) rich ... (REV 3:17-18; WORDS IN BRACKETS ADDED).

Jesus is talking about being "rich towards God", which, as the parable of the Rich Fool (Luke 12:13-21) shows, has no connection to material riches, except perhaps inversely. Earlier in 2 Corinthians, Paul describes his own ministry in similar terms: he was "(materially) poor, yet making many (really) rich" (6:10). Along with drinking Jesus' blood, eating the bread of life, waking from sleep and many other powerful images, getting rich (by buying gold!) is a metaphor for salvation and is not meant to be taken literally.

The consequences of misreading the Bible on the subject of poverty and riches are grave. To claim that the benefits of peace with God include health and wealth is an insult to tens of millions of Christians in the Majority World, who are not and may never be affluent, but may nonetheless be just as faithful to God and blessed by him as us, if not more so. Closer to home, it ignores the Bible's clear teaching on the dangers of greed and the freedom contentment brings. Further, it sets up false expectations so that when hardship or trouble of whatever kind comes, believers are not equipped to cope, and may become disillusioned with the faith. With tragic irony, the real problem with prosperity preachers is that in focusing on material benefits, they undersell the gospel of beneficial hardship and glorious hope that boasts in knowing and being known by God. *Caveat emptor.*

II

GREED
IS IDOLATRY

CHAPTER 3

SECRET IDOLATRY

THERE IS NO MORE serious charge in the Bible than that of idolatry. Idolatry called for the strictest punishment, elicited the most disdainful polemic and prompted the most extreme measures of avoidance. The theological grounds for the judgment of idolatry is the jealousy of God, which inevitably leads him to stern action: "You shall not go after other gods ... for the LORD your God ... is a jealous God, lest the anger of the LORD your God be kindled against you, and he destroy you from off the face of the earth" (Deut 6:14–15; cf. Josh 24:19–20; Ps 78:58–64; Zeph 1:18).

The crime of idolatry is mentioned in the Mishnah (the second-century AD rabbinical collection of the oral law) only to clarify the question of culpability and punishment.[1] The majority opinion accorded idolatry the punishment of stoning, the severest punishment of all, and it was ranked first of the three commandments which should never be transgressed by a Jew (the other two concerned illicit sex and bloodshed). That idolatry was not only threatened with severe punishment but also received it can be illustrated on a national level. One of the lowest points in Israel's history was the destruction of Solomon's temple, which Rabbi Yohanon ben Torta blamed on idolatry, illicit sexual relations and bloodshed.

In the Old Testament, disgust and contempt for idolatry are communicated by several derogatory terms used to describe the idols. Idols are 'unclean things', 'weak' or 'worthless things', 'that which is insubstantial', and a 'vanity' or 'emptiness'. The Israelites were not simply to avoid idolatry; the language of prohibition could hardly be more emotive and urgent; they are "to utterly detest and abhor" the heathen gods (Deut 7:25–26). For both Jews and Christians in the ancient world, the charge of idolatry evoked horror and alarm. The Church Father Tertullian (c. AD 200) did not exaggerate when he described idolatry as the "principal crime of the human race, the highest guilt charged upon the world, [and] the whole procuring cause of judgment".[2]

The equation of greed with idolatry

For this reason it is surprising to learn that the New Testament equates greed with idolatry on no fewer than four occasions. Colossians 3:5 states that "greed * ... is idolatry", and Ephesians 5:5 that the greedy person is an idolater. And according to Matthew 6:24 and Luke 16:13, Jesus portrayed wealth and possessions as a master that rivals God: "No one can serve two masters, for either he will hate the one and love the other, or he will be devoted to the one and despise the other. You cannot serve God and money [literally, Mammon]".

A possible fifth condemnation of greed in terms of idolatry appears in Revelation. In Revelation's announcement of the fall of Babylon, the economic and religious dimensions of her sins are not easily separated. The economic greed of Rome, to which the symbol of Babylon in the original setting of the book refers, has a peculiarly religious guise. The

---

* Or 'covetousness' as the ESV translates it.

harlot's cloth in 18:16–17 not only underlines Rome's extravagant luxury but also alludes ironically to the sacred garments of the priests in Exodus 28:5, 15–17. Likewise, the reference to Babylon deceiving the nations in 18:23 is evocative of the effect of idols on their worshippers. Finally, the counterpoint to Babylon's wealth is the spiritual wealth of the new Jerusalem in the following chapters, suggesting that there is more to the greed of Rome than meets the eye. It may be that Revelation 18, with its use of fornication language, condemns the influence of Roman imperial religion, alongside a forthright condemnation of Rome's economic exploitation of the Empire. Alternatively, the two emphases may be seen as inextricably bound together, with Rome's economic sins being portrayed in religious terms. Rome / Babylon may well represent the very embodiment of idolatrous greed.[3]

Is greed then idolatry? Can it really be that bad? Does the love of money really pose such a serious threat to God? What are we to make of these verses? Surely they are simply ill-considered exaggerations, or at best religious rhetoric designed to arrest our attention but not to engage our minds?

Is greed idolatry?

Greed and idolatry in the ancient world in fact had a lot in common. First, both focused attention on items made of gold and silver. In biblical and Jewish tradition these two metals are frequently associated with both the greedy, who can be called literally 'lovers of silver', and the idols of pagan worship, beginning with the golden calf. Secondly, both the greedy and the idolater visited pagan temples, the latter for obvious reasons, and the former since in antiquity the temples operated not only as places of worship but as banks.

And thirdly, both greed and idolatry, according to moral exhortation found in the New Testament, were considered to be of such gravity that they ought to be 'fled'; greed in 1 Timothy 6:11 and idolatry in 1 Corinthians 10:14.

In our day, whatever we make of the words of Jesus and Paul, it is worth noting that people with no religious commitment have observed the almost religious function money performs for many people. *The Oxford English Dictionary*, for instance, defines materialism in religious terms, as "devotion to material needs or desires, to the neglect of spiritual matters". Two articles in *The Times* went even further. Alexander Frean pointed out: "Bereft of employment security and increasingly detached from traditional faith in religion, people appear to have elevated material objects ... virtually to objects of faith".[4] Dorothy Rowe suggested that such devotion to material things is bound to fail: "Even if we achieve what the world is pleased to acknowledge as success, we discover that the seizing of it fails to satisfy the hunger of our spiritual expectation".[5]

As it turns out, the judgment that greed is idolatry is both an incisive social critique of modern society and a profound insight into Christian theology and ethics.

If the greedy are guilty of worshipping their money and possessions, what then is religion? There are many different answers to this question. Some define religion in psychological terms, stressing the notion of the holy or the sacred, and people's response to it. Others look at the functions of religion, such as the quest to make sense of the ultimate problems of life and the attempt to integrate people into social units or communities of faith. Still others take a more popular approach, noticing elements common to all religions, including belief systems, rituals, symbols and ceremonies.

No matter how it is defined, a good case can be made for concluding that greed qualifies as a religion.

There has never been a time in the history of the world when Jesus' and Paul's condemnations of greed as idolatry seemed more apt and made more sense than now. If people in the ancient world worshipped stocks and stones (Jer 2:27; Hos 4:12, KJV), today is everywhere to be found the worship of stocks and shares. Sociologist John Boli is not exaggerating when he warns:

> *We must come to terms with the depth of the problem [of materialism]: We are dealing with a highly institutionalised economic religion that must be confronted on its own terms, and many of the cultural underpinnings of that religion are, I believe, truly sacred to us all.*[6]

In Western society in general the economy has achieved what can only be described as a status equal to that of the sacred. Like God, the economy, it is thought, is capable of supplying people's needs without limit. Also like God, the economy is mysterious, unknowable and intransigent. It has both great power and, despite the best managerial efforts of its associated clergy, great danger. It is an inexhaustible well of good(s) and is credited with prolonging life, giving health and enriching our lives. Money, in which we put our faith, and advertising, which we adore, are among its rituals. The economy also has its sacred symbols, which evoke undying loyalty, including company logos, product names and credit cards.

People today conduct their lives primarily in terms of economic religiosity. The economy is the ultimate source of value and, as a religion, confers value on those who participate in it. Not to participate in the economy is to lack any social worth, as many of those without paid employment have come to learn.

As a religion, the economy supplies solutions to the basic puzzles of life and help in negotiating them. The meaning of a person's life is found in full participation in the economy, as both a producer and a consumer. The purpose of life involves the full development of the individual's economic potential and the pursuit of material progress for the good of all. Scores of books and courses are available at every level to assist the faithful to realize their potential. Whereas once the most vivid and intense experiences of life were to be found in traditional religion, today they involve money rituals, whether at work, on holidays or shopping. The religion of money even has its creeds and dogmas, such as 'Money makes the world go round'.

The modern-day equivalent of the city cathedral is the major shopping mall. The centre of the community in every sense, such complexes are admired for their huge, costly edifices and their awe-inspiring architecture, which often includes an aesthetically pleasing internal space made of glass and stone. They are visited by 'pilgrims' from across the country and sometimes even from overseas. Visitors spend hours in such places (not to mention loads of money), drinking in the experience of being overwhelmed by the variety and beauty of the goods on offer before returning to their local shopping centres and their everyday lives the better for it.

The fact that money has taken on religious significance for many people is clear from the British National Lottery. The twice-weekly draw is televised and watched by millions of people. It bears a remarkable resemblance to a church service. There is a leader of worship, musical items, personal testimonies (to the life-transforming power of money) and the holy sacrament of releasing the balls. One popular presenter was even known to offer a prayer: 'I know I'm a sinner, but make me a winner!'

Traditional religions saw the home as the place where instruction could be carried out most effectively. The religion of money is no different, with both television and computers inculcating the good news for every age group. The average American watches about eighty-five television advertisements each and every day, all of which relentlessly and unequivocally advocate an ideology of consumption and materialism.

The once noble occupation of the evangelist spreading the gospel has also been replaced by a secular alternative. Someone distributing religious tracts outside a shopping centre is today regarded with suspicion and looked upon with scorn. Yet we take for granted the legitimacy of the person making an appeal on behalf of this or that product.

Some denominations of the Mammon religion in America even had a wicked power to struggle against, namely communism, or the 'evil empire' as President Reagan used to call it. The demise of communism has cemented the associations of goodness and piety which such circles attached to capitalism and materialism. Dorothy Rowe rather cynically contends that all Americans believe in three things: God, America and the Market. Perhaps there is a sense in which the boundaries between these three entities have become blurred.[7]

Traditional religion does not stand a chance against this new religion. It has been pushed to the sidelines. Boli explains: "Religion may help us save our souls or understand the agony of life and death, but it cannot help us to obtain the vast array of goodnesses, meanings and purposes that are preferred in the economic realm".[8] Alan Storkey sounds a similar note of despair:

> *Christianity, despite all the warnings in the Gospels,*
> *has not even seen the challenge, the temptation, the*
> *lies, the enemy. We must consider sometime how*
> *completely the Christian community is unable to*
> *discern what is seeking to be the god of this age.*[9]

Some forms of Christianity have followed a time-honoured course in response to this newly ascendant religion: namely, syncretism, an attempt to cash in on the attraction of its beliefs and practices. The gospel of health, wealth and prosperity is the response of those who consider resistance to be of no avail. "If you can't beat 'em, join 'em." When such preachers proclaim that it is God's will for you to be healthy and wealthy, and that not to be so is evidence of your lack of faith, they fail to reveal only one thing: which god they are talking about.

Conversely, the much lamented but seldom resisted commercialization of the traditional religious festivals, such as Christmas, is a clear example of the takeover strategy of the religion of greed.

The most disturbing thing about the fact that greed is idolatry is that hardly anybody owns up to being a worshipper. Imagine the response of disbelief in the local church if it were revealed that the vast majority of its members were secretly worshipping other gods. Yet if our analysis of the religion of money is right, the unthinkable may not be so far from the truth.

The most convincing evidence that greed is idolatry concerns the answer to a simple question: what do idolaters do with their idols which believers are meant to do with God? The answer is that they offer their idols love, trust and obedience. In each case, that is exactly what the greedy do with their money. There are various ways to define greed. Greed is wanting more money and possessions. Greed is the opposite of contentment. Greed is a refusal to share your possessions. And so on. Our approach in the following three chapters is to consider greed in terms of its driving motivations. What causes people to be insatiable and mean with respect to material things? Greed is driven by inordinate love, misplaced trust and forbidden service; as such greed is rightly condemned as idolatry.

ENDNOTES

1. E.g. Mishnah *Sanhedrin* 7:4, 6–7, 10; 11:1, 6.
2. David W. Bercot, *A Dictionary of Early Christian Beliefs* (Peabody, MA: Hendrickson, 1998), p. 350.
3. Whether worship of the belly in Romans 16:18 and Philippians 3:19 refers to Jewish preoccupation with food laws or circumcision, fleshly egocentricism or gluttony and (by extension) greed, is difficult to say.
4. Alexander Frean, *The Times*, 5 September 1997, p. 11.
5. Dorothy Rowe, *The Times*, 1 September 1997, p. 34.
6. John Boli, 'The Economic Absorption of the Sacred', in Robert Wuthnow (ed.), *Rethinking Materialism: Perspectives on the Spiritual Dimension of Economic Behaviour* (Grand Rapids: Eerdmans, 1995), p. 95. My analysis of the religion of money builds upon that of Boli and Miroslav Volf (in the same volume).
7. Dorothy Rowe, *The Real Meaning of Money* (London: HarperCollins, 1997), p. 54.
8. Boli, 'The Economic Absorption of the Sacred', p. 113.
9. Alan Storkey, 'Postmodernism and Consumption', in *Christ and Consumption*, edited by Craig Bartholomew and Thorsten Moritz (Carlisle: Paternoster, forthcoming).

CHAPTER 4

INORDINATE LOVE

The New Shorter Oxford English Dictionary defines the verb 'to worship' as: "Honour or adore as divine or sacred, esp. with religious rites or ceremonies".[1] By this definition, the greedy clearly do not worship their possessions. *The Oxford English Dictionary's* 'transferred' (or figurative) sense for 'worship' is probably more helpful for our purposes: worship is to "regard with extreme respect, devotion, or love".[2] If to worship something means to have great love for it, then the excessive love of money, for which the greedy are known, constitutes idolatrous worship.

This is certainly the way the majority of biblical commentators have understood the assertion that greed is idolatry in Colossians 3:5 (cf. Eph 5:5). The Church Father Radalphus, for example, said: "God, for each one of us, is what we honour above all else, what we *admire and love* above all".[3] The Reformer John Calvin agreed: "[The greedy person] sets all his *heart* and mind on them [material things], and forgets God ... You see then that the covetous abuse their riches by setting *their whole heart* upon them".[4] And the biblical scholar J. B. Lightfoot adds: "The covetous man sets up another object of worship besides God. There is a sort of religious purpose, a *devotion* of the soul, to greed, which makes the sin of the miser so hateful".[5]

The love of money

Love may be a many-splendoured thing, the subject of count-less songs and works of fiction, but it is pretty diffcult to define. There is a world of difference between the romantic love of a couple, the fraternal love experienced in a football team and the compassionate love of the nurse or aid worker, let alone between divine love, parental love, patriotic love and so on. Love can arise out of all sorts of motives and emotions, including physical attraction, affection, pity, wonder, grati-tude and pride. You can love your spouse, your mates, the down-and-out, God, your parents and your country, not to mention your dog, your car, tomato ketchup and French mustard. Why and in what sense do the greedy love money?

In one sense the answer to this question is obvious enough. From the frenzied response to the glamorous prizes offered on the game shows which appear regularly on our televisions we may observe that if money can't buy love, most of us seem to think that it can buy happiness. Visible delight and palpable glee burst from the screens into our living-rooms as shining goods are dangled tantalizingly before per-spiring contestants. Sneering aside, there is no doubt that money can bring great pleasure and comfort. Only a desert monk would pretend otherwise.

Keep the Aspidistra Flying was George Orwell's cynical advice on such matters, offered in his 1936 novel by the same name. The main character, Gordon Comstock, an idealistic young man, gives up the material comforts afforded by his job in an advertising agency to work as a part-time bookshop assis-tant in order to pursue his passion for writing. Falling in love with Rosemary, Gordon blames his new-found poverty for his failure in matters amorous. He gives up poetry and returns to his former job, setting to work on their campaign to market a product which masks foot odour (PP, 'pedic perspiration', a slogan inspired by the analogous BO, body odour). Comstock embraces again the middle-class values of owning furniture and paying bills. These are quizzically symbolized in the potted aspidistra, an ugly house plant with broad tapering leaves. This plant, which he dubs 'the tree of life', was to be seen through the lace curtains of the front windows of many of the respectable and comfortable homes in his day. Having sold his principles for a piece of common flora, Comstock offered himself small consolation: "Everyone rebels against the money-code, and everyone sooner or later surrenders".[6]

While it is true that a lack of money does have its serious drawbacks, Comstock's devotion to money, which is enshrined on the title page of the Secker and Warburg edition of the novel, goes too far:

> *Though I speak with the tongues of men and of angels, and have not money, I am become as a sounding brass, or a tinkling cymbal. And though I have the gift of prophecy, and understand all mysteries, and all knowledge; and though I have all faith, so that I could remove mountains, and have not money, I am nothing. And though I bestow all my goods to feed the poor, and though I give my body to be burned, and have not money, it profiteth me nothing. Money suffereth long, and is kind; money envieth not; money vaunteth not itself, is not puffed up, doth not behave unseemly, seeketh not her own, is not easily provoked, thinketh no evil; rejoiceth not in iniquity, but rejoiceth in the truth; beareth all things, believeth all things, hopeth all things, endureth all things ... And now abideth faith, hope, money, these three; but the greatest of these is money.*
>
> I CORINTHIANS 13 *(adapted)*

We have to distinguish between the legitimate enjoyment of material things, which the Bible takes for granted and nowhere disputes ("God ... richly provides us with everything to enjoy", 1 Tim 6:17b), and an illegitimate and unhealthy attachment to wealth as an end in itself ("The love of money is a root of all kinds of evils", 1 Tim 6:10a). A number of Christian authors have attempted to draw this distinction. We will review the ideas of three, namely Augustine, David Clarkson and Martyn Lloyd-Jones.

The Church Father Augustine presents an understanding of idolatrous greed in terms of the notions of enjoyment and pleasure. According to Augustine, there is a distinction between those things which are to be enjoyed and those which are to be used: "To enjoy a thing is to rest with satisfaction in it for its own sake. To use, on the other hand, is to employ whatever means are at one's disposal to obtain what one desires".[7] The failure to observe this distinction results in sin: "Every human evil or vice consists in seeking to enjoy things that are to be used, and to use things that are to be enjoyed".[8] In the strictest sense, only God is to be enjoyed, and things are to be used as means to this end. Sin results when we enjoy things, in the sense of finding true and ultimate joy and satisfaction in them, and use God to procure more and more things. Thus the greedy are clearly guilty of idolatry in that they love money rather than God.

Justo L. González explains this Augustinian perspective:

The greedy seek to enjoy their possessions and sometimes even to use God in order to increase their wealth. In doing so, they fall into cruss idolatry, for only God is to be enjoyed and all things are to be used to attain that enjoyment.[9]

The Puritan David Clarkson once preached a sermon in London on the words 'Greed is idolatry', entitled 'Soul idolatry excludes men out of heaven', which is remarkably comprehensive and penetrating. Clarkson distinguishes between two sorts of idolatry: external, involving actions of the body, including bowing and prostrating oneself, which he describes as open and gross idolatry; and internal, consisting of acts of the soul, "when the mind is most taken up with an object, and the heart and affections most set upon it",[10] which he designates "secret and soul idolatry".[11]

Clarkson analyses the worship of the soul in terms of thirteen acts, and charges that "to give any one of them to anything besides the God of heaven is plain idolatry".[12] He argues that it is necessary to define clearly the proper worship of God in order to understand the idolatrous worship of the greedy. Ten of these so-called acts of worship develop the concept of the love of money. Indeed, Clarkson makes it clear that for him the heart of the matter is the question of love: "for wherein does the idolatry of covetousness consist, but in this? That it is an inordinate, an immoderate love of riches".[13]

The following summary draws on Clarkson's own language: God is, for every human being, that which (1) we most highly value or esteem; (2) we are most mindful of, be it profits and pleasures or God himself; (3) we most intend (our chief aim or purpose), whether to be rich, great and powerful or to glorify God; (4) we are most resolved for, whether lusts and outward advantages or God's ways, honour and service; (5) we most love and adore;[14] (6) we most fear (the loss of); (7) we most desire and enjoy, either worldly enjoyments or "spiritual communion with God"; (8) we most delight and rejoice in; (9) we are most zealous for, be it our own things or the things of God; and (10) we are most grateful for.

When later in the sermon he lists sixteen ways in which "men make wealth and riches their god", it is this idea of misplaced affections that he amplifies. Note the following verbs and phrases: the greedy value, love, desire, delight in, grieve over, are more affected by, eagerly seek and prize material things more highly than God. The breadth of Clarkson's definition of soul idolatry is matched by the size of the net in which he believes the guilty are captured:

> *Every natural man, let his enjoyments, privileges,*
> *accomplishments, be what they will, is an idolater ...*
> *[and] the greatest part of Christians.*[15]

Comparing this vast throng to Jacob (in Genesis 31), who denied the presence of idols in his possession, Clarkson asserts that "though few will own it [soul idolatry], nothing is more common".[16] This grim diagnosis continues in terms of the corruption of human apprehensions, thoughts, goals, supports, expectations, affections, elections, inclinations and fruitions, through the examination of which Clarkson aims to uncover "the guilt of this secret sin".[17]

Finally, the influential twentieth-century Welsh preacher Martyn Lloyd-Jones, although he did not use the terms 'love', 'devotion', 'heart' or 'affections', gave an explanation of greed as idolatry which nevertheless qualifies as a description of the inordinate love of the greedy for their possessions. Its value lies in the fact that the description works well in reverse: what the greedy do with money, they should rather do with God; hence the accusation of idolatry:

> *anything that you and I tend to set up as the big*
> *thing, the central thing, in our lives, the thing about*

which we think and dream, the thing that engages our imagination, the thing that we live for, the thing that gives us the biggest thrill, if it is anything other than God, it is idolatry.[18]

When the Bible condemns the love of money it does not expect us to turn ourselves into glum killjoys; things are to be heartily enjoyed as part of God's good creation. Nor does it call us to stop preferring one food over another (I love seafood and hate corned beef); desire leading to strong personal preference is beside the point. Rather, the love of material things is to be resisted when desire leads to a *consuming quest*. Tragically, many people's lives are characterized by such a quest from the cradle to the grave. What we politely call 'getting something behind us', 'moving up', 'becoming more comfortable' or 'improving our circumstances' is often just a thin disguise for the fact that we are "in love with this present world" (2 Tim 4:10).

The lust of the eyes

The Sermon on the Mount contains an enigmatic saying concerning the soundness of a person's vision:

The eye is the lamp of the body. So, if your eye is healthy, your whole body will be full of light, but if your eye is bad, your whole body will be full of darkness (MATT 6:22–23).

The key term for understanding these words is 'healthy', the Greek word *haplous*. It literally means 'single' and is used in the Greek Old Testament as a metaphor for undivided loyalty in the service of God. The point being made is that if you are focused on just one thing, obeying God, you will see where you are going and won't lose your way in life.

A related term is used in the New Testament with the connotation of generosity, and may well be intended here in view of the contrast with 'the bad eye' in verse 23, which can be used to express miserliness and stinginess. Perhaps a double meaning is intended, since both the themes of total devotion to God and detachment from material concerns are treated in the context of verses 19–21 and 24–34. These verses supply a sombre message worth pondering: the greedy will have divided loyalties and won't be able to see where they are going. They live without clear direction or orientation. They don't see things as they really are. Their entire person is in moral darkness.

Human desires are in fact often conceived of as involving the eyes. This is especially the case when the objects of desire involve food or the opposite sex. We chastize children who take too much food by saying that their eyes are bigger than their stomach. And our pupils dilate automatically at the sight of someone we find attractive. If the Bible sometimes describes sexual immorality as 'the lust of the flesh', greed can be said to be 'the lust of the eyes' (e.g. 1 John 2:16). Intriguingly, in Ecclesiastes the Preacher puts these two lusts in close proximity. He claims to have amassed for himself

> ... *silver and gold and the treasure of kings and*
> *provinces. I got singers, both men and women, and*
> *many concubines, the delight of the children of man ...*
> *And whatever my eyes desired I did not keep from*
> *them* (2:8, 10; cf. 4:8).

The link between sexual desire and the desire for riches is well known in our day and frequently exploited in advertising. Marketing for everything from swimming-pools to power tools employs the strategy. Such advertising plays on the viewer's desire to possess both the beautiful model and, by association, the product on display. Indeed, the essence of greed, like lust, is the desire to possess absolutely and exclusively.

Any approach to dealing with the love of money takes this into account. Some religious orders solve the problem by calling on their members to renounce all material possessions. At the other extreme, communism calls for private property to be abolished altogether in favour of state or communal ownership. The problem, however, is not that we as individuals *have* things, but that we hold on to them so tightly. Would you think you had 'lost everything' if in a fire you lost everything? In part, the Bible's solution to the love of money is to help us loosen our grip on our possessions and get a grip on something which far exceeds them in value.

Understandably, people tend to love things of lasting value. This is true not just of antiques and works of art, but also of cars, furniture, sporting equipment and shoes. Our favourite building materials are usually those that maintain their finish. Cheap materials in time devalue themselves. On the other hand, we condemn as immature our children's attachment to things which obviously will not last, such as fairground toys and the free gimmicks which come with children's fast-food meals. What is the point of loving something that is destined for the rubbish bin?

1 John 2:15–17 applies this logic to all material possessions: "Do not love the world or the things in the world ... [for] the world is passing away along with its desires". Likewise Paul advises "those who buy" to live "as though they had no goods", and "those who deal with the world as though they had no dealings with it. For the present form of this world is passing away" (1 Cor 7:30–31). Material things are not the last

word. The social and economic institutions which seem so important to us now have no ultimate permanence.

The purest forms of greed are based on a world view which does not acknowledge the world to come. The prospect of death has an inescapable logic for those who see it as the end of existence: get what you can, while you can. God recommends not world denial, but a recognition, along with the God-givenness of material things, of their inherent limitation and transience. In view of eternity, even top-drawer merchandise has an inbuilt obsolescence.

Loving God with your money

The Bible has much to say about love. It has one whole book which celebrates the beauty of love between a man and a woman. It narrates numerous romances, speaks of the love of good food, love of sound teaching and love between brothers and sisters, love for the nation and love for one's children. It also warns against certain kinds of love, including love of sleep, love of the flattering praise of others, and most frequently of all, the love of money. Its main reflections on love are, however, not negative but positive. The Bible commends love for God as the highest, purest, most ennobling and enduring form of love: "Hear, O Israel: The LORD our God, the LORD is one. You shall love the LORD your God with all your heart and with all your soul *and with all your might*" (Deut 6:4–5, my italics).

Israel's great Shema (as this passage is known), which Jesus referred to as the first and greatest commandment (Mark 12:28–31), and which was read daily (along with the Ten Commandments) in the temple in Jerusalem, receives an unusual rendering in the targums, the Aramaic paraphrases of

the Old Testament which were used in the first-century syna-
gogues. They offer a fairly literal translation of Deuteronomy 6,
with one striking exception. In verse 5 one targum has: "Now
you should love the Lord your God with your whole heart, and
(with your whole) soul, as well as with *all your possessions*" (my
italics). The Hebrew 'strength' is rendered by the word
'mammon', which means 'wealth' or 'possessions'. Two other
targums use the related term 'money'.[19]

Deuteronomy 6:4–5 expresses God's claim to our ultimate and full allegiance and a refusal to share this loyalty
with another. The Lord alone is our creator, redeemer and
judge, and as such calls for a total commitment in terms of
love. The rest of the chapter in effect elaborates on this
demand for exclusive loyalty to God. In this context it is
indeed striking that one of the loyalties singled out in early
Jewish interpretation as a threat to faithfulness to God
concerns wealth and money. Apparently, possessions were
considered a potent rival which could intrude upon and spoil
our love for God. It is not that love for money and material
things is somehow evil in and of itself. Rather, it is harmful
to us in that it robs us of something far better. The person
"who loves money will not be satisfied with money" (Eccl 5:10),
but the one who loves God will find satisfaction indeed.

ENDNOTES

1. Edited by Lesley Brown. Vol. 2: N–Z, p. 3723.
2. cf. *Oxford English Dictionary* (2nd edition, 1989), definition of an idol: 'Any
    thing or person that is the object of excessive or supreme *devotion* or that
    usurps the place of God in human *affection*' (vol. 7, p. 29, my italics). *Collins
    English Dictionary and Thesaurus* (Glasgow: HarperCollins, 1993), p. 1348,
    defines worship in similar terms as 'admiring love or devotion'.
3. Homily II.20 (*Patrologia Latina* 155, p. 2013), my italics.
4. John Calvin, *Sermons on the Epistle to the Ephesians* (Edinburgh: Banner of
    Truth, 1973), pp. 503–504, my italics.
5. J. B. Lightfoot, *Epistle to the Colossians* (London: Macmillan, 1904), p. 210, my italics.

6. *The Complete Works of George Orwell 4: Keep the Aspidistra Flying* (London: Secker and Warburg, 1987), p. 267.
7. Augustine, *The City of God* 11.25.
8. Augustine, *On Various Questions* 83.30.
9. Justo L. González, *Faith and Wealth: A History of Early Christian Ideas on the Origin, Significance, and Use of Money* (San Francisco: Harper and Row, 1990), p. 216.
10. Clarkson, *Works* 2 (Edinburgh: Banner of Truth, 1988), p. 300.
11. Clarkson, *Works* 2, p. 300.
12. Clarkson, *Works* 2, p. 301.
13. Clarkson, *Works* 2, p. 307.
14. Clarkson, *Works* 2, p. 302: "Love, whenever it is inordinate, is an idolatrous affection".
15. Clarkson, *Works* 2, pp. 305–306.
16. Clarkson, *Works* 2, p. 306.
17. Clarkson, *Works* 2, p. 313.
18. D. M. Lloyd-Jones, *Darkness and Light: An Exposition of Ephesians 4:17 – 5:17* (Edinburgh: Banner of Truth, 1982), p. 340.
19. Cf. the same targums to Proverbs 3:9, which have "Honour the Lord with your mammon".

CHAPTER 5

MISPLACED TRUST

WHAT IS THE FIRST WORD that pops into your head when I say 'money'? Many of us are familiar with the psychological test in which a person is confronted with a string of words and must in each case respond immediately with a single word. Supposedly the test can reveal the deep significance which you attach to something. What associations does the word 'money' carry for you?

Money means different things to different people. Money is everything from pleasure, comfort, contentment, freedom and fun, to filth, imprisonment, disgust and degradation. For a great many people money is, above all, security. Fear is a universal human emotion which all of us deal with every day. Fear breeds insecurity. One of the main ways in which we make ourselves secure for the future is by accumulating money. The very language of finance demonstrates this function of money. You can literally buy futures and securities.

There are basically two problems with putting our trust and confidence in money. First, God gets jealous. And secondly, it doesn't work.

The jealousy of God

In the Bible God is depicted, among other things, as a king. As king, he expects trust and confidence in his ability to provide for and protect his subjects. When the Israelites asked for a king of their own, God took it personally. In response to their request he asserted that "they have rejected me from being king over them", and he compared the offence to "forsaking me and serving other gods" (1 Sam 8:7–8).

When the nation of Israel felt under threat from hostile neighbouring powers, they did the sensible thing and entered into treaties for the sake of national security. Such treaties, however, were regarded by the prophets as nothing less than unfaithfulness to God. The nation was looking to Egypt or Assyria for help instead of to God. Isaiah chides the nation for her treaty with Egypt along these lines:

> Woe to those who go down to Egypt for help
> and rely on horses,
> who trust in chariots because they are many
> and in horsemen because they are very strong,
> but do not look to the Holy One of Israel
> or consult the LORD!
> The Egyptians are man, and not God.
> (ISA 31:1–3; CF. JER 2:18–19)

Ezekiel compares such treaties to the marital unfaithfulness we normally associate with idolatry:

> You also played the whore with the Egyptians, your
> lustful neighbors, multiplying your whoring, to provoke
> me to anger ... You played the whore also with the
> Assyrians (EZEK 16:26, 28).

The nation was not guilty of literally worshipping other gods, yet they are effectively charged with idolatry for trusting in a substitute for God. Idolatry in this sense is *an attack on God's exclusive rights to our trust and confidence.*

Trust and confidence frequently describe people's attitude to idols. The Lord describes the idols of the wayward Israelites in Deuteronomy as that in which they take shelter, the rock in which they sought refuge (32:37–38). The idol-worshippers in Isaiah 44:17 say to their idols: "Deliver me, for you are my god". And according to Habakkuk 2:18 the one who fashions an idol "trusts in his own creation".

Not surprisingly, the Bible accuses the greedy of this same form of idolatry. Psalm 52:7 speaks of the person "who would not make God his refuge, but trusted in the abundance of his riches". Proverbs 18:10–11 sets forth the same alternative: "The name of the LORD is a strong tower; the righteous man runs into it and is safe. A rich man's wealth is his strong city, and like a high wall in his imagination". And in Proverbs 28:25 a greedy person is contrasted with one who trusts in the Lord. Significantly, in the so-called 'psalms of trust' the two main alternatives to God as objects of trust are idols and riches (see Pss 115:2–9; 40:4; 62:8–10).

The call to trust in God and not money is also sounded in the New Testament. It is implied in the instructions to the disciples not to take any money with them when they undertake the work of mission (e.g. Mark 6:8–9), and in the calling of Peter and Matthew to leave all and follow Jesus (Mark 1:18–20; Luke 5:28). In 1 Timothy 6:17 the rich are warned straight out to trust not in their riches but in God. The parable of the rich fool in Luke 12:13–34 puts the lesson in the form of a story, and Jesus points to the birds and lilies, both of which trust God for their food and clothing, as examples to follow (Matt 6:25–34).

Trust and pride often go together. The wicked "trust in their wealth and boast of the abundance of their riches" (Ps 49:6). What we go to for security and protection is what we boast about. Hence 1 Timothy 6:17 calls the rich not to be arrogant, and in Luke 16:14–15 wealth is "exalted among men". Riches and arrogance are stable partners. The rich often appear to be smug, superior and self-satisfied. God's preference for the humble has to do with their readiness to trust exclusively in him.

No-one in the history of the church placed more importance on the judgment that greed is idolatry, and made more use of it in preaching, Bible exposition and theology, than Martin Luther. The foundation for Luther's understanding of greed as idolatry is laid in his treatment of the first commandment. What does it mean to have no other gods before the Lord? Luther defines worship broadly in terms of the idea of trust. In the catechisms which Luther wrote to nurture young Christians, he explains how to have no other gods before the Lord: we are to fear, love and trust God above all things. A god is that in which we put our trust and confidence. To obey the first commandment is, according to Luther, to cling to, rely upon and look only to God for whatever we need in any circumstance.

People have as a god that from which they expect to obtain help and comfort. Whereas faith is trust in God's help, unbelief is trust in oneself or one's own powers. In this sense, Luther insisted, unbelief and greed go and grow together. The greater the greed, the more unbelief, and *vice versa*. Sadly, material prosperity is often accompanied by loss of trust in God. The rich often think they simply don't need to trust in God. They have made other arrangements. Like the rich farmer in Jesus' parable, who says:

> *I will tear down my barns and build larger ones ...*
> *And I will say to my soul, Soul, you have ample goods*
> *laid up for many years; relax, eat, drink, be merry*
> (LUKE 12:18–19).

whom he calls a fool, each of us is prone to trust in his or her own resources.

Sin, for Luther, is always an act of contempt for God. It is significant for Luther that when Moses explains the first commandment, in terms of what causes someone to break it, he first of all mentions riches and luxurious living, which Luther interprets as mammon and greed:

> *when the LORD your God brings you into the land ...*
> *with great and good cities ... houses full of all good*
> *things ... and vineyards and olive trees ... take care lest*
> *you forget the LORD* (DEUT 6:10–12).

Trusting in riches prevents the human heart from being ruled by faith and love, and consequently the Lord is forgotten. For Luther, Moses himself understood the first commandment in a spiritual sense, as trust in God, and idolatry as a trust in things.

Whereas we uniformly regard some financial gain (be it a promotion, inheritance, profit, or whatever) as an unqualified blessing which cannot fail to put a smile on our face, the Bible contains many warnings which suggest that such windfalls can in effect be a curse. Deuteronomy 8:12–14, for example, indicates that prosperity may lead to pride, self-reliance and forgetting the Lord. Likewise, in Deuteronomy 32:10–15, newly acquired wealth is said to lead to abandoning God: the Lord cared for Israel, gave her the produce of the field, honey, oil, milk, the best cuts of meat and the finest of flour, only to watch the nation grow fat and self-satisfied, and eventually to forsake and scoff at him. Indeed, Proverbs 30:8–9 teaches that it is better to be denied wealth than to be wealthy and deny God: "give me neither poverty nor riches ... lest I be full and deny you and say, 'Who is the LORD?'"

Finally, in Job 31:24–28 both greed and idolatry are understood as involving trust in a substitute for God, and are said to constitute unfaithfulness to God. The greedy person, like the idolater, is guilty of misplaced trust. Job explains that if he had made silver and gold his trust or called fine gold his confidence, or if he had committed idolatry by worshipping the sun and the moon, both these sins would have constituted effective denials of the true God.

Many people recognize the dangers which money can pose. Most of us would regard £1 million in cash and an annual income of £250,000 to be a dream come true. 'I could live on that!' might be our wry and knowing response. The fact is that you could also die on it. The Duke and Duchess of Northumberland's son Percy was heading for this lump sum and annual top-up on his eighteenth birthday, via a trust set up in 1918 by the seventh Duke of Northumberland. When he reached fourteen years of age, the legal guardians of the fund voted unanimously to defer the inheritance until he turns twenty-five. Edward Davidson, the Duke's lawyer, explained that the decision had been taken in Percy's best interest: "He could harm himself very severely if he has a fund of this size. The Marquess of Bristol inherited a large sum of money on his 21st birthday and never recovered from it".[1] It is striking that the beneficiary of such 'good fortune' should be described as being in danger of 'very severe harm'. Apparently the marquess to whom the lawyer referred died from what his family described as 'chronic drug abuse'.

The futility of riches

The problem with being rich and thinking that you don't

need God is that you are wrong. The same goes for the person who worships an idol and expects to gain some benefit. Both greed and idolatry are not only wrong, but stupid.

One of the main premises of the biblical injunction against idolatry is that it is useless. Many pagans believed that certain benefits, such as fertility, rain and health, resulted from worshipping idols. Against this background, many Old Testament texts proclaim the ineffectualness and vanity of idolatry. The Bible ridicules idol worship, portraying it as powerless and deceptive. Such texts stress the perishable nature of the idols, their human origin in the mind and skills of the maker, and their lifelessness.

The worship of idols leads inevitably to the disappointment and embarrassment of those who trust in them. Habakkuk 2:18–19 is just one example:

> *What profit is an idol*
> *when its maker has shaped it,*
> *a metal image, a teacher of lies?*
> *For its maker trusts in his own creation*
> *when he makes speechless idols!*
> *Woe to him who says to a wooden thing, Awake;*
> *to a silent stone, Arise!*
> *Can this teach?*
> *Behold, it is overlaid with gold and silver,*
> *and there is no breath at all in it.*

Wealth is likewise ultimately unreliable and trust in riches useless. Proverbs asserts that wealth is fleeting and is not a firm basis for security: "Whoever trusts in his riches will fall" (11:28; cf. 18:11–12). The possibility of imminent death is also linked to the futility of storing up riches (cf. Ps 49:10–14, 16–17; Prov 10:2; 27:24; 28:22; Eccl 5:10–17). In Shakespeare's

Measure for Measure (III, 1) the Duke says to Claudio:

> *If thou art rich, thou'rt poor;*
> *For, like an ass whose back with ingots bows,*
> *Thou bear'st thy heavy riches but a journey,*
> *And death unloads thee.*

We can see this occasionally even today in the bizarre lengths to which the fabulously wealthy sometimes go to try to prolong their lives.

The richest centre of trade in the New Testament period was the city of Rome. The commercial interests of imperial Rome spanned the entire known world. For many under her rule, especially those who were not well off, the city was seen as the ultimate expression of unbridled avarice. And by rich and poor alike, her power was taken to be immense and her rule impregnable. Yet Revelation 18 prophesies the fall of Rome/Babylon, calling to mind the fall of Tyre, the greatest trading centre of the Old Testament period (which is prophesied in Ezek 26–28 and Isa 23). Those who stand to lose most from her demise are the focus of the account, namely, the kings (18:9–10), the merchants (18:11–17a) and (their employees) the seafarers (18:17b–19). These three classes of mourners are precisely the people who benefit directly from Rome's prosperity. They lament their lost sales in 18:12–13 ("cargo of gold, silver, jewels, pearls, fine linen, purple cloth, silk, scarlet cloth", and so on), the imported luxury goods which represent their crass extravagance. And in 18:14 Rome's self-indulgent opulence, ostentatious display and addiction to consumption are decried: her fruit, dainties and splendour are lost, "never to be found again". Such imagery makes the unreliability of riches abundantly clear.

Jesus pointed to moth, rust and thieves in Matthew

6:19–21 in order to underscore the precariousness of wealth. And the rich are advised in 1 Timothy 6:17 not to trust in the uncertainty of riches (but in the God who alone is immortal).

While death may still be around, some might suggest that money is today a far more stable and reliable form of security than in antiquity. And solutions have surely been found for the proverbial moth and rust! Isn't such talk simply out of date? In short, the answer is no. To think that money can provide security is to be deluded.

Money offers no protection against the vagaries of nature, the so-called 'acts of God'. So many things are out of our hands and can spoil our plans in an instant. Unemployment, war and natural disasters are only the tip of the iceberg. We used to say something was 'as safe as the Bank of England'. Yet the Bank of England has not been entirely successful at bringing economic stability and was powerless to save a bank as prestigious as Barings, for example. Pension funds are likewise not always what they appear. And insurance companies do not always pay up. Lloyds of London, which has the backing of the wealthy Names, seemed impregnable. Yet in the eighteen months prior to the meeting in the Albert Hall to discuss the crisis which threatened to undo Lloyds, thirty Names had taken their lives, in despair over their financial demise.

Natural disasters such as hurricanes, earthquakes, floods and tidal waves seem to be ever more frequent in our day. The north and south polar ice-caps are melting. The ozone layer is disintegrating. Major earthquakes and volcanic eruptions are expected in numerous densely populated areas. World population is exploding. And terrorists are becoming better armed. Such developments make the moth, rust and thieves of which Jesus spoke look pretty harmless when it comes to the threats they potentially pose to our possessions.

Another problem with seeking security through material acquisition is that other people notice our wealth, and the cost of security tends to spiral. Envy can lead to burglary and theft. The fear of such things leads many rich people to live in what amount to fortresses. Security without freedom is a good definition of incarceration.

Trust in wealth is, in the final analysis, a sad example of human folly. But worse than that, it is an insult to the Creator and Sustainer of the universe, who alone constitutes the sure ground for our confidence and trust.

ENDNOTES
1. *Daily Record*, 16 February 1999, p. 19.

CHAPTER 6

FORBIDDEN SERVICE

IN THE ANCIENT WORLD the institution of slavery was taken for granted. Most religions, including Judaism and early Christianity, employed the model of 'servant and master' to talk about how to relate to God. Few people questioned the assumption that almost everybody served somebody or other, whether God, one of the pagan gods or a human master. In the modern world, by contrast, we congratulate ourselves on the abolition of slavery and we prize our personal freedom. Slavery is thankfully a thing of the past. Or is it?

Unintentional servitude

In the Old Testament, a primary action of believers towards God, and of idolaters towards their gods, was service and obedience. Even in ceremonial contexts, the notion of serving the deity signified more than just isolated acts of cultic worship. When it is said that people served one of the gods such as Baal, or the Lord, the term implied not only the exclusive nature of the relationship but the total commitment and obedience of the worshipper. That worship involved service in the sense of submission to the will of a higher authority is clear from the phrase 'to bow the knee', which is used by Paul as a synonym for worship (Rom 11:4; 14:11; Eph 3:14; Phil 2:10).

Thus it is something of a puzzle when we read the words

of Jesus which claim that some people serve money (Matt 6:24; Luke 16:13). How is that possible? Some have suggested that Jesus was referring to a demon or god. In the nineteenth century a few scholars claimed that Mammon was a known Syrian deity, and in some post-apostolic Christian sources Mammon is depicted as the demon of wealth. Certainly Jesus believed in the existence of the Evil One and his cohorts, whose goal it is to tempt humans to disobey God. There is no convincing first-century evidence, however, for a firm link between greed and a demon or god. A better explanation is that Jesus' words, "You cannot serve God and money" (Matt 6:24), personify wealth as an evil and superhuman power which distracts people from serving the true God. It was a well-known insight not only among Jesus and Christians, but also among Greeks and Romans in general, that wealth could exercise an enslaving power.

No-one sets out to become a slave of money, and most people do not recognize their servitude until it is too late. People wrongly assume that money is serving them. Several authors have noticed this cruel irony. The Church Father Cyprian (died 258), Bishop of Carthage, wrote of those

> who add forests to forests, and who, excluding the poor from their neighbourhood, stretch out their fields far and wide into space without limits ... Such a one enjoys no security either in his food or in his sleep. In the midst of the banquet he sighs, although he drinks from a jewelled goblet; and when his luxurious bed has enfolded his body, languid with feasting, he lies wakeful in the midst of the down; nor does he perceive, poor wretch, that these things are merely gilded torments, that he is held in bondage by his gold, and that he is the slave of his luxury and wealth rather than their master.[1]

The English philosopher and lawyer Francis Bacon (1561–1626) agreed:

> *If money be not thy servant, it will be thy master.*
> *The covetous man cannot so properly be said to possess*
> *wealth, as that may be said to possess him.*[2]

And the French theologian and ethicist Jacques Ellul stated: "We can, if we must, use money, but it is really money that uses us and makes us servants by bringing us under its law and subordinating us to its aims".[3]

The tragic and pitiful figure of Ebenezer Scrooge, in *A Christmas Carol* by Charles Dickens, represents well the slavery which greed imposes. In an encounter concocted by the Ghost of Christmas Past, Scrooge is confronted with the awful truth that he worships a golden idol: "I have seen your nobler aspirations fall off one by one, until the master-passion, Gain, engrosses you". As a younger man "there was an eager, greedy, restless motion in the eye, which showed the passion that had taken root, and where the shadow of the growing tree would fall".[4] To his surprise, it is made clear to Scrooge that what he needs is nothing short of 'release' from his captivity.

A nineteenth-century hymn by Joseph Barnby tells the story of the Macedonian man's cry for help (Acts 16:9–10), a vision Paul received on his second missionary journey to take the gospel from Asia Minor into Europe. Whereas the first two verses of the hymn expand the call taking Macedonia as a symbol for fallen humanity (for example, "How mournfully it echoes on! / For half the earth is Macedon; / These brethren to their brethren call / ... 'O ye that live, behold we die!'"), the third verse takes pains to stress that, paradoxically, the world as a whole neither issues nor hears the call. "By other sounds the world is won / Than that which wails from Macedon". According to the hymn, the world "cannot list the alien cry". The cause of people's indifference to their need of God is put down to greed: "The roar of gain is round it [the world] rolled, / Or men unto themselves are sold". Not only does the clamour for more drown out the cry from Macedon, but humans are depicted as in bondage to these very lusts.

Serving Mammon

Slavery to money can affect those at every level of society, and may even be thought of as encompassing society as a whole. It has its grip on people at every socio-economic level. But worst of all, it can cause people to act in hard, unfeeling and even self-destructive ways, as the Church Father John Chrysostom brought out in his frequent references to the judgment that greed is idolatry.[5]

Chrysostom explained the equation in terms of forbidden service. Above all, Chrysostom felt the shocking rhetorical impact of the words, and sought with all earnestness to impress them upon his hearers. He insists that to call greed idolatry is no exaggeration, but in fact "pure truth". Greed, according to Chrysostom, is "an illness of the soul", "the worst type of decay". He expects his hearers to "shiver" and "shudder" at Paul's words and to "flee from this decay and seize the imperishable". With preacher's licence he goes as far as to say that greed is "worse than idolatry"; the greedy person is "much worse than an idolater" because, whereas idolaters defend their form of worship, the greedy happily condemn in others the thing they themselves worship.

Chrysostom believed that the greedy are guilty of idolatry because they serve and obey something other than God. Anticipating the objection of the greedy that they do not worship their money, he counters:

> *Do you deny it [the charge of idolatry] because you do*
> *not kneel in front of it? You are bowing much lower*
> *before it by your works, and that constitutes greater*
> *servility. In order to recognize this, look upon God and*
> *tell me: Who worships him more? Those who only*
> *stand praying before him or those who do his will?*
> *Obviously the latter. Thus those who do his will, serve*
> *mammon more diligently.*

For Chrysostom, the fact that the greedy serve their own self-ish desires comes out in several ways. He claims that the "altar of greed ... strongly smells of human blood", implying that the greedy oppress the poor and needy in their relent-less drive for more. With reference to Cain, who "wanted to cheat God due to greed", he explains that greed leads to a lack of love, and eventually to pride and even "hatred and contempt of fellow human beings". The unstated premise in Chrysostom's interpretation is that since greed demands behaviour that involves disobedience to God, then such serv-ice involves "falling away from God" and thus may justifiably be called idolatry. In order to lead the greedy to repentance, he stresses the goodness of God in creation in supplying human needs and "an inheritance in heaven", a far superior form of riches (a strategy we will explore in chapter 8).

One of the great problems with money is that the more you earn the more you spend. If you ask people how much is enough, most of us, if we are honest, will answer, 'Just a bit more'. No matter where we are on the salary scale, people tend to look enviously upon those just above them. What we forget is that those people do the same thing with the ones on the rung above, and so it goes on.

Those who do, by all accounts, earn enough are often trapped in work that harms their quality of life. Why is it that people stay in jobs which clearly damage their health, their general well-being and their families? The answer is they are in slavery. They simply cannot accept a job on lower pay, because people, naturally enough, match their lifestyle to their income. And it does not take long to get used to a better income. Most people literally could not afford to accept a lower income.

Family therapists report that, when counselling families in need, you can ask the adults to consider the way they are treating each other, how they relate to the children, and so on. Such questions usually evoke little resistance. If you ask whether an adult needs to work so long and hard or might consider a different job, however, the responses range from intransigence to incredulity. Consider the experience of one counsellor:

> *I was talking to a guy recently—he and his wife were having troubles with their daughter—we talked about that and that was fine, and then we were talking about what the difficulties were and that was fine, and we were getting on and then it came around to how much of the problem was dad, and dad was working fifteen hours a day, seven days a week. People were ringing him up in the middle of the night and things like that. He looked physically ill. He said, "It's just the work", and I said, "Well, can't you cut it down? It doesn't look to be doing you much good". He said, "Yes, but I've got to keep going at it". I said, "What if you just say that's it, forget it, I'm going somewhere else". He said, "I did that last year and they just put my pay up by 25 per cent and how do you walk away from that?"[6]*

Such a tale does seem to approximate to a modern form of

slavery. It is indeed a rare person who can make a decision which reduces his or her income. Many of us are slaves rather than masters when it comes to our money.

In the light of this, and in order to understand such self-destructive behaviour, it is tempting to conceive of greed as an addiction. Addiction is among the most tragic things that can happen to you or a loved one.[7] Whereas the pleasures gained from drugs and alcohol are seldom denied, those who become addicted to such substances can find themselves and those around them in deep despair. In a society that teaches that we are our own creators, there are few more frightening scenarios than losing control of oneself. From all appearances, the addict is bound by a pattern of destructive behaviour laced with obsession and delusion.

The dynamics of addiction are well known. What starts out as a pleasant habit escalates to a point where decidedly unpleasant after-effects lead to deteriorating relationships and withdrawal from worthwhile activities. Preoccupation leads to obsession and compulsive behaviour; excuses lead to denials, delusions and self-deception. Others are drawn into the web of addiction to support and enable, perhaps unwittingly, the whole debilitating process. Finally, the addict can truthfully say that there is no choice; the addiction is in charge.

Addiction is a syndrome which gives us an insight into what can happen with so-called appetitive sins like lust, gluttony and, in particular, greed. It would be an exaggeration to label greed an addiction. It may be fair to say, however, that addiction is greed with the volume turned up. Much of what is true about the spiral of addiction could, to a lesser degree, be said of those who create and resent the bondage of greed. Many could identify with the addict's sense of confinement, futility and lack of choice when it comes to money matters.

As minor addictions go, greed is able to injure and disfigure in frightening ways.

Some secular analysts have made observations of the economic behaviour of entire societies which basically amount to the accusation that all of us suffer under a form of economic slavery. In offering his comprehensive critique of capitalism, Karl Marx at one point employs the rhetoric of idolatry. His reflections are not, of course, concerned with the interpretation of the New Testament. We don't normally look to Marx for help in understanding the Bible. In fact, in his discourse the counterpoint to idolatry is not the true worship of God, but rather human self-fulfilment. Nevertheless, what he says constitutes an unwitting interpretation of the words 'greed is idolatry' which extends Chrysostom's ideas from the level of the individual to the whole of society.

Marx reflects on the irony of the capitalist system, as he saw it, wherein, instead of products belonging to their producers, the reverse state of affairs obtains, and alienation results. Products are no longer valued for their usefulness, but only for their market value. Money becomes the alien god that confers this value:

> Money is the general, self-sufficient value of everything. Hence it has robbed the whole world, the human world as well as nature, of its proper worth. Money is the alienated essence of man's labor and life and this alien essence dominates him as he worships it.[8]

Marx asserted that greed has a dehumanizing effect:

> The more the worker exerts himself, the more powerful becomes the alien objective world which he fashions against himself, the poorer he and his inner world become, the less there is that belongs to him.[9]

In Marx's view, greed is a god because it dominates people's lives and demands an obedience tantamount to slavery. Marx views greed not as a matter of individual morality but as a structural and societal ill. We do not need to subscribe to his political ideas to see the disturbing kernel of truth in what Marx says.

Why is greed such a powerful urge that people and whole communities are taken over by it, to the extent that they end up serving and obeying money? It has to do with placing too high a value on material things. People use money to bolster their sense of existence. In short, to recall the previous two chapters, when it comes to money, many of us suffer from inordinate love and misplaced trust. What is needed is a different way of thinking about ourselves and a new appreciation for the things which are not seen. More will be said on this in the next three chapters.

Slaves of sin

Both in much theology and in the popular mind, sin is thought of in terms of guilt. The solution to sin is, then, forgiveness. This is of course right and proper. It tells only part of the story, however—one third, to be exact. Sin is not only guilt but also ignorance and a power. God solves all three problems for us sinners through the death and resurrection of Jesus Christ.

What did the cross achieve? First, the cross saves sinners, dealing with our guilt (Rom 5:1–11). Jesus bore the penalty for our sins so that we might be forgiven and have a right standing with God. Secondly, the cross tells us about God, dealing with our ignorance. At the cross we learn of God's strict justice (Rom 3:21–26) and amazing love (Rom 5:8).

Thirdly, the cross conquers evil, dealing with our bondage and impotence: through the cross God "disarmed the rulers and authorities" and "put them to open shame, by triumphing over them" (Col 2:15).

It is this third aspect of sin and salvation that is often neglected and has keen relevance to the forbidden service of money. Sin blinds and binds. We need not only forgiveness and true knowledge of God but liberation and deliverance, which is what the word 'salvation' really means. But we can't begin to experience this freedom until we acknowledge our bondage. Too many of us are so busy making ends meet that we fail to notice the chains that bind us. The Germans have a saying: "Money is a good slave, but a bad master".

ENDNOTES

1. Cyprian, *Epistle* 1.12, my italics.
2. Cited in Solomon Schimmel, *The Seven Deadly Sins* (New York: The Free Press, 1992), p. 165.
3. Jacques Ellul, *Money and Power* (Southampton: Marshall Pickering, 1979), p. 76.
4. Charles Dickens, *A Christmas Carol* (Oxford: OUP, 1988), pp. 38–39.
5. Chrysostom, *Homilies on Galatians, Ephesians, Philippians, Colossians, Thessalonians, Timothy, Titus and Philemon* (Grand Rapids: Eerdmans, 1979). See especially the 18th homily on Ephesians.
6. Reported in Dorothy Rowe, *The Real Meaning of Money* (London: HarperCollins, 1997), p. 148.
7. Much of the following discussion builds on chapter 8 of Cornelius Plantinga, *Not the Way It's Supposed to Be: A Breviary of Sin* (Leicester: Apollos, 1995).
8. Karl Marx, *Writings of the Young Marx on Philosophy and Society* (New York: Doubleday, 1967), pp. 245–246. Moshe Halbertal and Avishai Margalit, *Idolatry* (Cambridge: Harvard University Press, 1992), p. 43, explain Marx's view further: 'The more man works the more he accumulates money, and the more he externalizes his essence to the alien god of money.' See also Stanford M. Lyman, *The Seven Deadly Sins: Society and Evil* (New York: General Hall, 1989), pp. 253–259, on Marx's characterization of money as 'omnipotent ... like a god' (p. 254).
9. Marx, *Writings of the Young Marx on Philosophy and Society*, pp. 289–290.

III

LEARNING
CONTENTMENT

CHAPTER 7

CONTENTMENT AND
THE KNOWLEDGE OF GOD

ALMOST EVERYONE AGREES that contentment is a good thing. The attractions and benefits of the contented state are obvious. Not to be content is a virtual synonym of unhappiness. And to say, 'I am content', is as positive an assessment of a situation as many people are ever willing to give. Indeed, the person experiencing the highest bliss can be described as 'filled to his or her heart's content'. To be content is to be satisfied, to enjoy a balance between one's desires and their fulfilment. To be content is in effect to experience freedom from want.

Whether you are content is more important to your well-being than how well-off you are. The Puritan Jeremiah Burroughs quaintly illustrated this point with reference to the activity of walking. He compared one's heart and one's material possessions to a person's two legs. How well you walk depends less on the length of your legs than on their being even in length. The person with two short legs is far better off than someone with one long leg (being rich and powerful) and one even longer leg (having a proud and insatiable heart).[1]

The fact that contentment is the opposite of greed and the solution to it is clear from the admonition in Hebrews 13:5: "Keep your life free from love of money". How, we might ask? The verse continues: "be content with what you have".

These six words form one of the most difficult commands

in the Bible, especially in our day of ingrained consumerism and unquestioned materialism. The world's approach to achieving contentment is by way of addition. "If only I could get such and such, then I would be satisfied", or so we tell ourselves. We are like the child who climbs a hill and sees a higher one in the distance, and thinks that from there it will be possible to touch the clouds. Once on top of that hill, we discover that we are just as far from the clouds as before. "The world is infinitely deceived in thinking that contentment lies in having more than we already have".[2]

But how are we expected to keep our wants in check when the economy to which we belong is driven by efforts to contrive new wants and dress them up as needs? Since the Second World War, succeeding generations in the West have accommodated their material expectations to what they have attained, whether in terms of the size of their dwellings, their luxuries and appliances, or the money they spend on leisure pursuits like overseas holidays.

To limit yourself voluntarily is a modern-day heresy, which, if discovered, is greeted with bemusement if not disbelief. The mortgage lender finds it hard to fathom a customer who does not apply for the maximum loan permitted by the size of his or her annual income. Virtually no-one is satisfied with what he or she has; few willingly forgo what they could afford. 'Enough' is always just over the horizon, and the horizon recedes as we approach it. To switch metaphors, so many of us are like the caged hamster running furiously in the wheel and getting nowhere, "trapped in the endless cycle of work and spend, whose poles mutually reinforce each other".[3]

Like greed, contentment is not only an intensely practical matter which can affect the way we live our lives almost every day, but one which has a profound theological basis and implications.

Contentment and knowing God

The Christian approach to contentment, like the Christian approach to virtually every subject, begins with the knowledge of God. The Christian faith supplies three good reasons to be content: first, because God himself is content; secondly, because he promises his people a secure future; and thirdly, because we can trust his goodness.

God's contentment

As odd as it sounds, there is a sense in which God is the contented God. He does not go for everything he can get. We are so used to talking about his infinite knowledge, power and presence that we often forget that in creating and in redeeming us he limited himself in acts of extraordinary self-control. We are not pantheists, believing that God is everything, but theists, holding that God has created and sustains the world but is independent of it. In doing so, the infinite God restricted himself in order to give a measure of freedom to his creatures.[4] Furthermore, he could have gone on creating, but instead stopped after six days.

Likewise, Christ, in becoming a human being, "made himself nothing, taking the form of a servant" (Phil 2:7). As Paul explains, "though he was rich, yet for your sake he became poor" (2 Cor 8:9). Along with praising God for his infinity, then, we do well to remember his humility.

God takes the lead in self-limitation. And in asking us to be content, he is no hypocrite. Since God was willing to limit himself, we should be ready to follow his example. When he calls us to "be content with what you have", he cannot help but shake his head in disappointment when we steadfastly refuse his advice. We entirely fail to appreciate the point of view from which it was issued. He is not like the medieval baron who expects his serfs to be satisfied with dry bread, while all the time he himself sups on the finest cuisine and has not the faintest inkling of what it means to do without.

God's promised future

A proven way to put up with uncomfortable restrictions is to set your mind on your wonderful destination. I am convinced that this is the only way people on long-haul flights are able to bear their many hours of intense discomfort. The same is true of Christians who willingly put up with less than they could afford or with less than they would like to have. Limitations can be borne, if it is clear that they are not permanent.

To cite an extreme example, it is reported that some of the early Christian martyrs found contentment in their sufferings using this logic: "Though we have but a hard breakfast, yet we shall have a good dinner, [for] we shall very soon be in heaven".[5]

In a similar fashion, Paul considers his "slight momentary affliction" to be far outweighed by "an eternal weight of glory" being prepared for him (2 Cor 4:17). Paul's troubles, which included imprisonments, days adrift at sea, sleepless nights, cold and exposure (2 Cor 11:25–27), to mention only his travelling accommodation, were neither light nor momentary by any other measure. Christ was able to bear even the pain and shame of the cross "for the joy that was set before him" (Heb 12:2).

In all these cases the restrictions were entirely voluntary and avoidable. The martyrs could have opted for a better 'breakfast' (by denying Christ), Paul for more salubrious quarters (by sticking to his trade) and Christ for heavenly glory (by foregoing the cross). Christians are uniquely able to be content; as Jeremiah Burroughs put it, "they see heaven before them and that contents them".[6]

Or it ought to. It should at least take the edge off our yearning for more now, and ease our disappointment at what we take to be material limitations in the present.

The ultimate incentive to contentment is the confidence that God is on our side, and is looking after us. The injunction in Hebrews 13:5 backs up its call to contentment with the words, "for he [God] has said, 'I will never leave you, nor forsake you'". In the original Greek, these words of comfort from God include no fewer than five negatives; they could hardly be more emphatic. We might paraphrase them: 'I will never, ever, under any circumstances ... fail to be there for you.' He will stick around no matter what happens.

Christians may be content because we have God. Burroughs explains:

> A godly heart enjoys much of God in everything he has, and knows how to make up all wants in God himself ... The saints in heaven do not have houses, and lands, and money, and meat and drink, and clothes; you will say, they do not need them—why not? It is because God is all in all to them immediately.[7]

No matter what the material circumstances on earth, such a heart can say to itself, "The LORD is my portion" (Lam 3:24). God is worth more than anything the world can offer. This is surely what Paul had in mind when he says that he has "learned ... to be content ... through him who strengthens me" (Phil 4:11, 13). As the old saying goes, 'It's not where you live that matters, it's who you live with.'

God's goodness

Contentment is rooted in trust in the goodness of God. As Christians, we believe that God knows best how to order things and that he has our best interests at heart. We affirm the universality and comprehensive nature of God's providence. Nothing takes him by surprise or escapes his notice. He knows all about us and is always with us. This does not exempt us from working hard and attempting to improve our lot. But it ought to give us a quietness of spirit to accept our circumstances when things don't turn out as we had hoped.

If we truly believe that God is good, we ought to make a favourable interpretation of his dealings with us. It is a tiresome friend who takes everything you say and do the wrong way and is always looking for fault. A good friend is someone who believes in you, and thinks the best of you even when appearances may at times indicate otherwise. We owe God such friendship. Do you feel that you are missing out in some material sense? If you have a clear conscience as regards your own laziness and wrongdoing, and you are left only to turn to comfort in God's will, hold fast to your confession that he knows what he is doing. It is worth remembering that to be given up to your heart's desires may be a dreadful thing (Ps 81:11–12; Rom 1:24, 26, 28). Perhaps he is preparing you for some work of service, or is saving you from some temptation that would destroy you. Perhaps he knows that you would not in fact be 'better off' if you were better off.

The value of contentment

Contentment is in no sense an isolated issue, but is intimately bound up with a host of virtues and vices. It can save a person from a multitude of sins and sets off a chain reaction of blessing that keeps on running.

Contentment requires patience. This applies both to waiting for the life to come, and to living sensibly in this life. We don't have the house, the car, the computer or the clothes we want, or whatever it may be, often because we are waiting for some improvement in our circumstances. The real tragedy of being discontented is that in longing for what we don't have, we cease to take pleasure in what we do have. We become frustrated at the child who refuses a nourishing and tasty breakfast cereal, just because the box containing his or her favourite is empty. All too often, adults mimic this childish behaviour, albeit in more sophisticated ways. A Jewish rabbi wisely stated: "Who is rich? He who rejoices in his portion".[8]

Unfortunately, patience is surprisingly difficult to achieve. When Paul prays for the Colossians to be "strengthened with all power according to his glorious might" (1:11), it is not so that they may perform some superhuman feat, but so that they may have the least impressive and most mundane of all the virtues, namely, 'patience'. In a Bible study, the group was asked which of the fruit of the Spirit (Gal 5:22–23) they needed the most help with; to a person, they all settled on patience.

When preaching on contentment, the Puritan Thomas Manton rightly observed that "patience is rooted in humility, but discontent in pride".[9] It is when we think we deserve better that we become discontented. From company executives to visiting professors, whether it concerns free accommodation or complimentary meals, the level of complaint concerning their quality and speed of delivery, which is very often high, is a fair measure of their pride.

By contrast, it is when we consider that 'God has dealt graciously with me', giving me more than I actually deserve, that we can say with Jacob (who said this when he was faced with a decision that would cost him materially), 'I have enough' (Gen 33:11). Those who think more highly of themselves than they ought find it hard to say, 'Enough.'

Just as discontentment gives off the scent of pride, it reeks of ingratitude. Grumbling is regarded in Scripture as nothing less than rebellion against God. Such attitudes are simply inappropriate for Christians who profess to be dead to the world's fading allurements, and alive to the eternal God, whose lives do not consist of their material possessions but are hidden with Christ in God (Col 3:3). It is no accident that Paul's exposition of what this implies for our lives on earth reaches its pinnacle in a threefold call to give thanks:

> *be thankful ... singing psalms and hymns and spiritual songs, with thankfulness in your hearts to God. And whatever you do, in word or deed, do everything in the name of the Lord Jesus, giving thanks to God the Father through him* (Col 3:15–17).

Our contentment arises not from getting the things which we want, but from God's fashioning our spirits to our condition, and from our recognizing his gracious provision, both spiritual and material.

The modern Western world view, ever since the Enlightenment, has been constructed in individualistic terms. Since capitalism promotes the unrestrained drive for personal increase, this by definition waters down any sense of community—which causes a myriad of social problems. Whereas the successful entrepreneur is often proud to stand alone, the essential nature of God is in relationships, both between Father, Son and Spirit in the Trinity and with human beings. The great theologian Karl Barth considered the notion of relationship to be central to the very idea of humans being created in the image of God: "male and female he created them" (Gen 1:27).[10]

If people are going to relate, they have to limit themselves. This applies as much to members of a household, or to castaways on a desert island, as it does to members of a society and even to the world community. When God supplied his people with manna in the wilderness, he instructed them to collect only their share and no more, "according to the number of the persons that each of you has in his tent" (Exod 16:16). This limitation was to prevent some from going hungry because of others' greed, a principle endorsed by Paul in the context of the Corinthian Christians' contribution to the collection for the poor saints in Jerusalem (2 Cor 8:15). The Lord Jesus taught us to pray, "Give us this day our daily bread" (Matt 6:11), not "Give us this day enough to hoard for many days to come".

Limitation for the sake of relationship is also the obvious motivation for the Bible's controversial prohibitions on lending at interest.[11] For us, interest is a legitimate payment for servicing a transaction which empowers someone to buy something now rather than later. Nothing could be more natural and convenient. Yet Deuteronomy 23:19–20 ("You shall not charge interest on loans to your brother") and Luke 6:35 ("lend, expecting nothing in return") take a radically different view. If Old Testament teaching was intended to protect the poor and vulnerable in the Israelite community (the Israelites could exact interest from foreigners), Jesus' instructions transcend the distinction between brother and foreigner, being set in the context of loving one's enemy, doing good and lending with a generous spirit (see Luke 6:32–36).

The terms used for 'interest' tell a story of their own. The

Old Testament has three words in Hebrew, which don't shrink from calling a spade a spade: *neshek*, which derives from the word for 'serpent' and means 'bite', refers to the paying of interest from the debtor's point of view; and *marbît* and *tarbît*, meaning 'increase', which see the transaction from the angle of the creditor. The Old Testament forbids 'biting' a fellow-Israelite in order to add to one's stockpile (to risk an unappetizing mixed metaphor). By contrast, we have invented a more civilized and wholly positive term for debt, namely 'credit'.

Some parts of the world see interest in an entirely different light. In 1985 a Brazilian labour leader referred to interest as a weapon more deadly than the atom bomb.[12] Third World debt puts the lie to the essential amorality of lending at interest. Without questioning the altruism of the World Bank, the IMF and the banks of the First World nations, it is no exaggeration to say that many nations today bear tremendous burdens due to their obligations to pay interest on the money they owe. For example, fully one third of Tanzania's budget each year goes on paying its loans. Whether or not empowerment was the intention, these loans have led to the very opposite.

We must, of course, tread carefully in applying the Bible's teaching on usury to our own day. It referred originally to simple lending and borrowing in agrarian communities. Changed economic conditions can't be ignored.[13] Yet at the very least, these texts embody the principle of being satisfied with getting less than one could, for the sake of others.

Indeed, contentment is the essential prerequisite for giving. It is a common fallacy to think that my ability to give hangs more on how much I earn than on my state of contentment. No matter how much I earn there will always be something to spend it on, unless at some point I am satisfied with what I already have. Money will always be in short supply, if I am not content.

When we are content, we exercise faith, humility, love, patience, wisdom and hope. Contentment prepares us to receive mercy and to undertake acts of service. It delivers us from an abundance of temptations. If greed is a hideous sin, contentment is a supreme grace which honours and pleases God.

Satisfied pigs?

Yet it is possible to have too much of a good thing. When it comes to contentment, this is definitely the case. As one author in the seventeenth century put it, "many are contented out of mere stupidity".[14] What they want matches what they have simply because they lack ambition or imagination. It is hard to argue with John Stuart Mill, who famously wrote: "It is better to be a dissatisfied Socrates than a satisfied pig".[15]

Just as contentment does not rule out ambition, but rather only the selfish and consuming variety, so too it precludes grumbling, not crying out to God for relief from genuine financial distress. Burroughs conceded: "Though a Christian ought to be quiet under God's correcting hand, he may without any breach of Christian contentment complain to God".[16] There is nothing commendable or spiritual in being satisfied in a monetary situation which does your dependants harm, if there is something which can be done about it. Christians are to be content, yet resourceful and hard-working, not indolent or irresponsible.

A second and even more squalid form of inappropriate contentment also involves taking it to an extreme. Christians ought to be at one and the same time the most contented and yet dissatisfied people in the world, for they want something this world cannot offer:

> *Godliness teaches us this mystery, Not to be satisfied*
> *with all the world for our portion, and yet to be content*
> *with the meanest condition in which we are ... A little*
> *in this world will content a Christian for his passage,*
> *but all the world, and ten thousand times more, will*
> *not content a Christian for his portion.*[17]

Ultimately, we are not satisfied to wallow in the mire, no matter how resigned to it we might appear. We long for a truly better place (and I don't mean the nicer part of town!). Our hearts are to be set on things above, not on the things of the earth.

ENDNOTES

1. Jeremiah Burroughs, *The Rare Jewell of Christian Contentment* (1648; Edinburgh: Banner of Truth, 1964), p. 46.
2. Burroughs, *The Rare Jewell*, p. 46.
3. Miroslav Volf, 'In the Cage of Vanities: Christian Faith and the Dynamics of Economic Progress', in Robert Wuthnow (ed.), *Rethinking Materialism: Perspectives on the Spiritual Dimension of Economic Behaviour* (Grand Rapids: Eerdmans, 1995), p. 171.
4. Cf. David T. Williams, 'Against the Tide: Christian Self-limitation', *EQ* 70.3 (1998), pp. 248–249.
5. Burroughs, *The Rare Jewell*, p. 83.
6. Burroughs, *The Rare Jewell*, p. 84.
7. Burroughs, *The Rare Jewell*, pp. 65, 67.
8. *Aboth* 4:1
9. Thomas Manton, *The Complete Works* (Worthington, PA: Maranatha, n.d.), 2, p. 313.
10. Karl Barth, *Church Dogmatics* (Edinburgh: T. and T. Clark, 1958), 3.1, pp. 181ff.
11. See Susan L. Buckley, *Usury Friendly: The Ethics of Moneylending – A Biblical Interpretation* (Cambridge: Grove Books, 1998).
12. Cited in Timothy Gorringe, *Capital and the Kingdom: Theological Ethics and the Economic Order* (London: SPCK, 1994), p. 139.
13. See Paul Mills, *Interest in Interest: The Old Testament Ban on Interest and its Implications for Today* (Cambridge: Jubilee Centre Publications, 1993).
14. Burroughs, *The Rare Jewell*, p. 33.
15. Quoted in Wuthnow (ed.), *Rethinking Materialism*, p. 179.
16. Burroughs, *The Rare Jewell*, p. 21.
17. Burroughs, *The Rare Jewell*, p. 43.

THE SECRET OF CONTENTMENT
Tony Payne[*]

I WAS FANTASIZING THE other day, in one of those moments between 2 and 3 in the afternoon when one should be working but isn't, what would happen if one of our TV magnates were converted, and decreed that his network's programming would hereafter reflect Christian principles.

In the few brief weeks before all the advertisers departed and financial ruin descended upon the network, what would happen to our favourite programs? They might be more honestly titled for a start. The National News might become instead *Largely Irrelevant but Entertaining Trivia to Keep the Days Apart*. Come to think of it, nearly all the programs could be given that title.

Some programs on the new Christianised channel would no doubt be axed immediately—*Temptation Island*, *Big Brother* and *Jerry Springer* come to mind. Others would need a make-over. I'm thinking particularly of the lifestyle programs, such as *Money* (hereafter called *Lucre*, with the subtitle: *How to earn it honestly and then give it away*.)

In this short-lived expression of genuinely Christian television, I would particularly look forward to the new version of *Better Homes and Gardens*. It would become a five-minute program called *Perfectly Adequate Homes and Gardens*. Each week, a former bricklayer or plumber would take us on a tour of a bog-ordinary family home, and say, "As you can see, the Wilson family home has plenty of potential. There's lots we could do with this one. However, it does the job pretty well. It's warm and dry and comfortable. No obvious structural problems. We're going to encourage the Wilsons to be content and leave it as it is." Cut to closing credits.

That such a program seems absurd is testimony to the extent to

---

* Originally published in *The Briefing*, #282.

which we have all accepted the premise of *Better Homes and Gardens*, and all the lifestyle programs of that genre—namely that of course we all want our homes and gardens to be better, our wealth wealthier, our health healthier, and our sex sexier. We all want what political parties routinely promise before elections: 'a higher standard of living'.

This constant desire for more and better is perfectly consistent with the atheism that pervades our society. (I don't mean the taxing theoretical atheism that requires real thought and some intellectual courage, but the lazy, practical atheism that most of our contemporaries adopt without thinking much about it). If this world is all that exists, and our own personal happiness within it is the best we can hope for, then we will always be looking to improve some aspect of our lifestyle to achieve the elusive happiness that we desire.

Accordingly, discontentment is our constant companion. We are never satisfied, and ruin the good that we do possess by demanding that it be better. And this is not only in regard to material possessions. If our wife is no longer good enough, or is not making us as happy as she once did, we trade her in, and get a newer model. If our work is frustrating us or not delivering the personal fulfilment we desire, we change jobs, or seek promotion. If the husband and children that we once thought would make our life complete now seem a drudgery and a drag, we run away and call it liberation.

Discontentment with our circumstances is entirely consistent with atheism; indeed, it is almost its logical consequence given the nature of the world. Since the world is very often a nasty and unpredictable place, and the people who inhabit it are equally nasty and unpredictable, personal happiness is elusive, and when attained, often short-lived.

Moreover, even though, Christianly speaking, the good gifts of creation are designed to bring joy, and are to be received with thanksgiving, this depends to a large extent on us receiving and using them according to the Creator's purposes. Thus, even though the pagans do enjoy and derive some happiness from the goodness of creation, even then they constantly undercut their

---

own happiness by rejecting the will of the Creator. They misuse and distort the good things of creation because of their rebellion against the Creator, and thus curtail their own joy.

Secret knowledge

Contentment is every bit as much the fruit of Christianity, as discontentment is of atheism, because the Christian already possesses the most precious thing in the universe.

The Apostle Paul makes this point quite stunningly in his letter to the Philippians. In chapter 3, he describes his impeccable personal credentials—of the tribe of Benjamin, a Hebrew of the Hebrews, and so on—and then says:

> Whatever gain I had, I counted as loss for the sake of Christ.
> Indeed, I count everything as loss because of the surpassing
> worth of knowing Christ Jesus my Lord ... (v. 7).

Compared with the treasure that is knowing Christ—or rather being known by him—everything else is secondary. Christ has made Paul his own, and so forgetting what lies behind, Paul presses and strains forward towards the goal, which is the upward call of God in Christ Jesus, the full possession of the 'citizenship of heaven' which is already his spiritually, and will one day also be his bodily (Phil 3:12-21).

All this is background to the famous passage on contentment in Philippians 4:

> ... for I have learned in whatever situation I am to be content.
> I know how to be brought low, and I know how to abound.
> In any and every circumstance, I have learned the secret of
> facing plenty and hunger, abundance and need. I can do all
> things through him who strengthens me (PHIL 4:11-13).

The 'secret' of contentment that Paul speaks of is not some trick of positive thinking. The Greek word translated 'secret' is a technical term for initiation into the inner secrets and knowledge of a mystery religion (in fact, the stem of the word is the same as for *musterion*, the 'mystery' of the gospel that Paul often refers to). Paul has been initiated into a new and hitherto undisclosed understanding that allows him to be quite content, whether he has abundant possessions or next to nothing. And what is that new and secret knowledge? It is, of course, Christ Jesus himself, who has made Paul his own, given him a righteousness by faith, and granted him peace with God and citizenship in heaven. It is Christ Jesus, whom Paul now knows as his Lord, who strengthens him in all circumstances to be content.

This knowledge of Christ, this peace with God through him, dispels anxiety and replaces it with joy and contentment, whatever our earthly circumstances. Because God has won the victory through Christ, we can now enjoy true peace with him, in all its eternal glory. In the equally famous passage about prayer (in Phil 4:4-7), the image is of this peace of God standing like a sentinel outside our hearts and minds, guarding them from anxiety, as we bring our requests to him.

In Christ, our desires are satisfied, ultimately and completely. In knowing Christ, we know him whom kings and prophets and angels longed to know, in whom are all the treasures of wisdom and knowledge, and all the riches of heaven. Once we know him, fluctuations in our earthly situation are of little moment. We can tolerate poverty, and our heads are not turned by abundance. We can be content whether we are single or married, slave or free, circumcised or uncircumcised (cf. 1 Cor 7:17-35).

In other words, contentment does not mean grudgingly tolerating a second-best existence. It means being completely satisfied because we truly have enough. Paul has learned the secret of contentment, because he truly has everything he needs. His desire is satisfied, because he knows the surpassing worth of Christ, compared to which everything else is nothing.

Paul's contentment is very different from the calm resignation of the Stoics, whereby one simply accepts misfortune because it is fate. His contentment springs not from pretending that the desire for joy and happiness doesn't exist—but in having it completely satisfied by his knowledge of Christ. (This is basically the point that John Piper has been making for many years in his books.) Precisely because of the inestimable worth of knowing Christ and being known by him, Paul's desire for earthly improvement has been relegated to the status of indifference. He can put up with poverty, and put up with abundance. Either way is fine by him, because he already has everything he wants or needs.

Striving to be different

The obvious question is: Why, then, are we Christians so often just as discontent as our pagan neighbours? Why are we also so upwardly mobile, so desiring of improvement in our house, our job, our schools, our cars, our food, our education, our possessions? Why do we, too, run after all these things? Why do we grumble and complain about our circumstances, and our general lot in life?

The simple answer is that we forget the secret. Having sold everything to buy the most precious pearl in the world, we pop it in a drawer and forget about it. We take our eyes off Christ, and become preoccupied instead with our earthly circumstances. Thus we struggle and strive for trinkets and trivia, rather than for Christ. For Paul, contentment didn't mean sitting back and doing nothing. Indeed, Philippians 3 paints a vivid picture of Paul being dissatisfied with his own imperfection, and pressing forward, with all his energy, to what lies ahead for him: the upward call of God in Christ Jesus (3:12-14). He was discontent with his own ungodliness, but utterly content with his earthly circumstances, whatever they happened to be.

We know in theory that this is how we, too, should live. Yes, Christ is the most important thing, and we shouldn't be too worried about our earthly ups and downs. We know that. But keeping that knowledge clear in our minds and hearts, when there is so much to distract us from it—that's the challenge.

Interestingly, and I think not accidentally, Paul's closing exhortations to the Philippians in chapter 4 have precisely this effect: they keep us strongly focused on what we possess in Christ and his heavenly kingdom, and thus, more content in any and every circumstance. Note how Paul exhorts them:

to rejoice in the Lord always (4:4); that is, to thank God and be glad at all times, knowing that the ups and downs of our current circumstances will not change the reality of our eternal circumstances, our citizenship in heaven;

to not be anxious but to pray (4:5-7); given that God's peace has been won for us through Christ, and that he cares for our every need, we can approach him about anything, and express our trust in his goodness towards us;

to focus their thoughts on what is just, pure and excellent (4:8); the way to avoid being preoccupied with earthly and unimportant matters, is to fill our thoughts instead with things that are good, right and pure, all of which come from God.

to put into practice the apostolic teaching they have seen in Paul's life (4:9); this is the daily effort of remembering and putting into practice the words of the Scriptures, and imitating those who provide us with an example of how it's done.

All these have the effect of focusing our hearts and minds on Christ Jesus, and increasing our knowledge of him. They lift our eyes to him, and to our citizenship in heaven, from where we await the Saviour's return.

That, or rather he, is the secret of contentment.

THIS PRESENT AGE: OUR STRUGGLE NOT TO COVET
Phillip Jensen*

> *As for the rich in this present age, charge them not to be haughty, nor to set their hopes on the uncertainty of riches, but on God, who richly provides us with everything to enjoy. They are to do good, to be rich in good works, to be generous and ready to share, thus storing up treasure for themselves as a good foundation for the future, so that they may take hold of that which is truly life* (1 TIM 6: 17-19).

Money. We're to enjoy it, but not to love it. There is nothing wrong with being rich, but wealth is a great snare. We are to receive all good things with thanksgiving, but at the same time build up our riches in heaven. It seems that a right attitude towards wealth is a constant balancing act between extremes, and there is no one level of wealth which is ideal; being rich may lead to self-satisfaction, being poor might make you resentful. How on earth are we to know whether we have the right, Christian attitude towards money?

The passage above from 1 Timothy 6 is a good place to start talking about riches, for here we have encapsulated the great blessings and the great dangers of wealth. Wealth does tempt us to be haughty. Wealth means other people will serve us; and it is very natural to become arrogant towards others when you know they'll do whatever you want. Wealth generates confidence, for it seems as if you will always be safe. Banks, insurance agencies and financial management companies all tell us the same thing: wealth is the way to make the future secure, so you can have peace of mind as well as comfort now.

In fact wealth does not give security, for it can disappear overnight, as survivors of stock-market crashes can testify. All wealth, whether inherited or earned, is a gift. The family into which

---

* Originally published in *The Briefing*, #280.

you were born, the economy, the time in history—all these are a gift from God. At this time in history, to be born into an Australian family means the possibility of a wealth not even dreamed of by most Afghan families.

But wealth is not wrong; God provides it to be enjoyed. This is part of using wealth well—as is being generous and using wealth to store up treasures in heaven. The last point is crucial: whether we are rich or poor materially, our real wealth is spiritual. That is the wealth we should value; that is the wealth on which we should judge ourselves. That is the wealth that matters. And in having this attitude towards money, Christians are at odds with the atheistic world, and also with other religions.

Material realism but not materialism

The secular world is materialistic. It believes philosophically that this life and this physical universe is all there is; and so it is not surprising that it preaches a doctrine of amassing material wealth. What else is there? There is no other ultimate justification, no other reward, nothing else worth having. The best we can have is material comfort, so we might as well devote everything towards that end. It is an entirely self-centred view, and for that reason it is terribly anti-social. Westerners care about the country's economy only because it affects their own wealth. Other people's interests might be addressed to the extent that together we can all create more wealth for ourselves; but other people do not really matter. There is a story circulating that some American business people, on seeing the planes crash into the World Trade Centre, reached for their telephones to sell shares. Whether or not this is true, the sad thing is we can well believe it could be true. We can easily imagine people whose immediate attitude to disaster is to think of how it affects their money. We can easily imagine it, because we could do it too.

Christianity is not the only religion to oppose this self-centred materialism, but it does it in an unusual way. Buddhism and the philosophies of Hinduism, for instance, are anti-materialist both philosophically as well as practically. Their doctrines teach that this physical world is not just passing, it is essentially an illusion—an evil illusion. Reality is found when the illusion of material existence can be overcome. This is done through denial, through asceticism and meditation. The physical world must be rejected entirely.

Christians, however, believe in creation. The material world is good, because God created it to be good. It is the doctrine of demons to reject the material world, to live in asceticism and denial of the generous gifts God gives us. Material things are good. Stereos and big houses and harbour views are good. Large salaries are good. It is better to be rich than poor, it is better to have food and clothes and beautiful things than to be without them. Poverty is not a godly state and money is not the root of all evil—although the non-Christian world generally thinks that we preach that.

No, the *love* of money is the root of all evil. You cannot serve both money and God. In serving God, however, money is a great thing to have. It is useful to consider the advice given to the exiles in Babylon, in Jeremiah 29:1-9. Build houses and live in them, God told them. Plant gardens and eat their produce, marry and have families. Even more, seek the welfare of the city and pray to the Lord on its behalf, for in its welfare you will find your welfare.

We are in exile, in the spiritual Babylon while we wait to get into the Promised Land, our spiritual Jerusalem. We should never forget Jerusalem; but while we are here, we should go about the business of living. The exiles in Babylon were tempted in two directions: to undermine Babylon as the enemy, or to enjoy living there so much they forgot Jerusalem. God told them to do neither. We have exactly the same two temptations: denial of this world or denial of the next. Well, in theory we do. Most middle-class Western Christians are in no danger of asceticism. Our danger is all the other way.

Paul tells us, in Philippians 4:11-13, that he has learned the secret of facing both plenty and hunger. With the power of God, he has learned to overcome the temptations of both. He has learned not to covet, which is the real evil at the heart of both riches and poverty. He has learned not to envy his neighbour, not to live in enmity with others who might have more. He has learned by the power of God to be content. How might we learn the same thing? How can we beware of the greed in our hearts?

The rule is simple: don't covet—but the material circumstances that go with coveting can be anything from billionaire-hood to utter poverty. Just about any action, from buying a lolly to selling a mansion can be done in a greedy manner—or a godly one. It is up to us to examine our own hearts. But there are things that, at least, should make us pause and do some re-examination. I have noticed recently a few clarion-call indicators which we should take as a signal that materialism may have moved in quietly and taken hold. The first issue, gambling, is one on which most Christians probably agree; after that we will get to the touchier ones— children's education and minister's salaries.

Gambling

The basic rule for Christians is, no gambling. This is not because there is anything inherently bad about games of chance—but then, the essence of gambling is not chance, but covetousness. Gambling is wanting something for nothing. It's wanting something that you don't have, that you want to take from someone else without paying for it. It almost inevitably involves taking somebody else's money. It doesn't feel like it, when the organizing body orchestrates the money exchange; but the money you win from a lottery, or a bet, or a marketing competition effectively comes from the other people who also want the prize. If none of you were so covetous, there would be no prize.

But what about sport? What about winning a trophy? What about investing on the stockmarket? There are a thousand different applications of gambling, some of which seem quite innocent.

What about when a company offers you a free food processor if you ring up and leave your address? They're going to give it away anyway! In all these things, the evil is covetousness. If you need a food processor, go and buy one. God is quite capable of providing you with a food processor. He can give you the money, or provide a Christian friend who will give you one. By participating in the 'competition', you are encouraging the system whereby people are motivated by their greed to read a company's advertising. Greed is the evil.

Of course, some activities can be practised without gambling. You can invest in the stockmarket in order to support a certain company that produces goods that help society. Or you can gamble on the stockmarket, investing without caring what the business is as long as it will increase your money. You can go and watch horseracing if you happen to like watching horses run. You can even play a game with yourself or a friend to see who can guess which horse will win. That is still different to betting on a horse. No doubt every reader can think now of an exception to these claims. It is the attitude of the heart that creates a gamble; the odds are irrelevant.

Schooling

How to divide your church in one easy lesson: preach on whether you should send your children to private or public schools.

Recent debate on schooling in New South Wales has produced some interesting definitions regarding the difference between public and private schooling. The private school, it is said, is the place where you bond. It's a close, protected environment where children make strong relationships with the other children, who will most likely be from similar backgrounds. Parents send children there because they want the child to bond with that group, for intellectual, cultural, religious or social reasons.

Public schools, on the other hand, force children to bridge.

Because the other children could be from any background or socio-economic group, children have to learn how to relate to different kinds of people. They must be able to build bridges across social gaps and form friendships with those from different backgrounds.

Of course it is not as clear-cut as that. Private schooling may involve some necessary bridging. Public schools generally draw children from one suburb, which in itself will involve a similar socio-economic background. A small public school in a country town may comprise children of more diverse backgrounds—although, of course, they will all have in common being country children. A school experience where real bridging with a totally different social group takes place is very rare.

Christian parents want to protect their children (as do almost all parents). They are also prepared to make sacrifices for the sake of their children. Parents also generally want their child to have a quality education, which is achieved most often in schools with small classes and many resources—private schools. Some also want their children to receive an explicitly Christ-centred education at a Christian school. These may be good reasons to send children to a private school. The question for parents is—are they actually the reasons that motivate you?

For as well as any such noble motivations as described above, private schools will also set your child on the upwardly mobile track to economic success. The other children they bond with will be the future high earners, so your child is likely to be up there with them. It tends to be the private schools that give the high marks that lead to entry into the good universities which lead to the profitable careers. In short, private schooling for children can very easily be a Christianised way of loving money. It may be for your children instead of yourself, but it's still a form of materialism.

It is not good for a country to have all its education controlled by the state. The freedom of choice in education is a necessary part of freedom of life. But we must not let our children's education become a way to indulge in love of money. There are so many ways in which a good cause like this—children and their education—can be twisted by our covetous hearts. For many people, private schooling is prohibitively expensive, so parents sacrifice home time for work in order to afford the schooling. But education is ultimately a parent's responsibility, and it requires relating to the children. Parents can make themselves so busy providing for their children that they have no time to know their children. Is private schooling really worth that?

Of course we want to provide good things for our children. It may be time, however, for some to pause and take stock. What are we buying for our children? What do they actually need? Love of money can appear anywhere, even in our love for our children.

Clergy salaries

Another issue which can fall prey to materialistic thinking is how much we should pay someone to minister the gospel.

Consider a minister in a poor suburb. Everyone in the suburb lives in three-bedroom fibro houses. The minister wants to fit in with his people. The church organisation he works for, however, has a standard policy for ministry salaries and housing. So they build him a brick rectory—the only brick house in the suburb—and pay him about five times what his neighbour earns. His congregation just can't relate to him. They're jealous of his wealth and feel uncomfortable being entertained in his house.

Consider the minister a few suburbs away, in a very wealthy area. He's paid the same salary, but in this suburb it gives him a house a quarter the size of his neighbours. When he entertains people, they can't believe how shabby the carpet is. He makes his decisions according to bus timetables. He never goes to the same restaurants, plays or concerts that his congregation members do. His congregation simply cannot relate to the way he thinks. He seems to be a walking insult to them all the time, not someone whose message might be listened to.

We must be able to reach people. In impoverished areas you simply cannot maintain nice middle-class standards and still do your ministry well. Missionary societies have known this for years—missionaries to impoverished areas are generally prepared for the fact they will probably have to reduce their standard of living. But ministers in Sydney, for example, still get their big brick houses in the 'fibro' suburbs. On the other hand, gospel ministry can be just as damaged by insisting on poverty in a rich suburb as it can by living in luxury in a poor suburb.

How do we live by the gospel with greedy hearts in this fallen world? Only by the power of God. We must work at learning the art of contentment. We must learn to live amongst riches without being seduced by the love of money, and in poverty without resentment. Some ministers will earn more than others will, even more so as our society becomes more diverse economically. What every minister should earn, however, is as much as he needs to live. Then all are equal whatever the suburb.

In the end, the salary is not what creates a problem of greed amongst clergy; sinful hearts create greed. We do not want a situation that haunts some areas of the United States, where ministers angle for rich ministries in order to grow rich. Neither do we want an equality of pay so rigidly enforced that no-one has what he or she needs. Ministers must always beware of the love of money. Do not covet more than you need. We have been given immeasurable riches in the kingdom of God. Be satisfied with them.

IV

SHARING POSSESSIONS

CHAPTER 8

THE SIGNIFICANCE OF GIVING
IN THE EARLY CHURCH

MOST PEOPLE IN OUR society tend to regard giving as a purely private business and approach it with the utmost care and the strictest calculation. Whereas we might spontaneously splash out on something special for ourselves when shopping, tight reins are kept on the sober activity of sharing our possessions. And few of us think of our enhanced ability to give when, on those rare but memorable occasions, news of a hefty pay rise brightens up our day. For most of us, giving is an ideal opportunity to exercise rigorous self-control and restraint. 'What's mine is mine' is so obvious that it hardly seems worth saying.

Giving and contentment are two sides of the same coin. Together they represent the positive alternative to greed. If contentment calls a halt to the *grabbing* dimension of greed, giving addresses its *keeping* aspect. Like contentment, giving turns out to be far more central and significant to Christian living and identity than might first appear. In this chapter we will consider not the practicalities of giving, which vary enormously between individuals and cultures, but the centrality of giving in the fight against greed. In order to accomplish this task we will, among other things, need to take a close look at the meaning of some key New Testament words and concepts, including 'greed', 'hospitality' and 'almsgiving'.

Identifying the greedy

Good detective novels or television series are often hugely popular, perhaps because so many of us enjoy the challenge of sorting through the suspects and picking out the guilty party. If the crime were greed, though, how would we go about pinning the blame?

Who are the greedy? The problem with defining the word 'greed' in the New Testament is that the relevant words appear mainly in lists of sins to be avoided, which supply little context or clue to their meaning. Naturally enough, commentaries and lexicons seek to give the words a meaning which justifies their appearance alongside the likes of murder, maliciousness, haters of God and inventors of evil, as in Romans 1:28–30, for instance. 'Wanting to get rich, avarice', simply doesn't seem wicked enough, at least to modern Western sensibilities. Hence definitions often include the adjective 'ruthless' and associate the concept of greed with dishonesty, violence and oppression. Thus people can be accused of greed only when their behaviour entails hurting others or compromising their integrity.

Simply wanting more wealth, however, was considered a vice by early Jews and Christians, and there were other words which carried the stronger meanings. The fact that 'greed' can signify just wanting to get rich, irrespective of the means employed, is suggested by the existence of Christian teaching which condemns just that: "Be on your guard against all greed"[*] (Luke 12:15); "Do not lay up for yourselves treasures on earth" (Matt 6:19); "Those who desire to be rich fall into temptation, into a snare" (1 Tim 6:9).

One place in the New Testament where 'greed' appears in

* Or 'covetousness', as in the ESV.

an illuminating context is Luke 12, where the parable of the rich fool gives no indication that the greed being condemned involves anything other than the accumulation of wealth by legitimate means (his land 'produced a good crop'). There are no firm grounds to conclude that greed is condemned only when it leads to other sins, as convenient as it might be to imagine otherwise. This seems to make the task of identifying the greedy unwieldy, to say the least. How many of us do not want to get rich?

So far, I have suggested that the greedy are those who love money inordinately (chapter 4), trust money excessively (chapter 5), serve money slavishly (chapter 6) and are never satisfied with their possessions (chapter 7). These four definitions could leave the impression that greed is at worst a personal and private sin, which is difficult to recognize in others. Love and trust, for instance, are among the most secret of emotions, to which others have little access without our consent. You might think that I am acting out of love for someone or trust in something, but you could be seriously mistaken.

While we may be accustomed to thinking of greed as a private and intangible vice, this was apparently not the case for the early church. The list of offenders in 1 Corinthians 5:10–11, who are to be excluded from the congregation, includes perpetrators of five very public and concrete offences, namely the sexually immoral person, the idolater, the slanderer, the drunkard and the swindler. There would be plenty of witnesses to pick this lot out of a line-up. The behaviours which characterize them were for the most part public and social. By definition, you can't be a slanderer or a swindler without involving someone else. But, the list also includes the greedy person, who presumably was just as visible and identifiable as the other five. Otherwise there would have been little point in including this offender in the list. How was the greedy person to be recognized?

We may surmise that the greedy in the early church were those who refused to "do good ... to those who are of the household of faith" (Gal 6:10; cf. 1 John 3:17), or believers who did not share their food with those who had less to eat at the community meals (1 Cor 11:20–22). In the early church the greedy were probably identified in the first instance as *those who refused to share their possessions*.

The opposite of greed

Greed put in danger the social harmony of the early church, which was by and large made up of close-knit communities. We need only consider the marked social dimension of the moral teaching of the New Testament, with its frequent 'one another' teaching ('love one another', 'serve one another', 'bear one another's burdens', and so on), the description of the shared communal life of Christians in Acts and the use of kinship language throughout the New Testament (believers address each other as brother or sister).

In the second century, Christians became known not for their doctrinaire pronouncements or political astuteness, but rather for the way they shared their possessions with one another in the community.

Lucian of Samosata, a pagan travelling lecturer and rhetorician with no direct interest in Christianity, supplies remarkable confirmation of this assertion. He comments incredulously on the eager willingness of Christians to support their travelling delegates "at their own expense ... for in no time they lavish their all". His explanation stresses Christian belief in resurrection:

The poor wretches have convinced themselves, first and foremost, that they are going to be immortal and live for all time ... Therefore they despise all things indiscriminately and consider them common property, receiving such doctrines traditionally without any definite evidence. So if any charlatan and trickster, able to profit by occasions, comes among them, he quickly acquires sudden wealth by imposing upon simple folk.[1]

It is clear from Paul's speech to the Ephesian elders at Miletus that giving is the opposite of greed. At the end of the speech (Acts 20:32–35), Paul draws attention to the fact that during his ministry in Ephesus he worked at his trade so that he would not be a financial burden to the Ephesians ("I coveted no one's silver or gold or apparel") and so that he might be in a position to support 'the weak' with money that he had earned. He cites "the words of the Lord Jesus" to support the latter point. The saying is commonly translated as comparing the states of the giver and the beneficiary: "It is more blessed to give than to receive". This sentiment, however, seems rather odd. Did Jesus really intend to cast aspersions on the blessing of receiving by comparing it unfavourably with that of giving? Most of us would affirm that as good as giving is, receiving is not that bad either.

The word 'to receive' can also mean 'to take hold of ', and in this context this makes better sense. The 'receiving/taking' which is being unfavourably compared to 'giving' is not that of the needy who are being supported, 'the weak', but rather of the ones who have worked and have the opportunity of sharing their possessions and pass up the opportunity. Paul is saying it was better for him to share his possessions than to keep them all to himself. The Jewish moral tractate Tobit (second century BC) makes a similar point: "It is better to give alms than to treasure up gold" (12:8b). Acts 20:35b might be translated: "It is more blessed to give than to keep".

The significance of giving

When we think of giving, it is usually in terms of money, and more specifically coins or notes dropped into an offertory plate or container. The main terms we use are 'charity' and 'donation'. The situation was quite different in the early church, where giving more often took in not just money but possessions generally, and was characterized more concretely as 'hospitality' and 'almsgiving'.

The New Testament notion of hospitality had nothing to do with impressing your friends at a dinner party in the hope of enjoying a nice meal in return. Rather, it consisted of *concrete, personal expressions of Christian love to fellow-believers.* It served as a positive practice to counter and expose greed.

Hospitality took a number of forms. It included meeting the pressing physical needs of the local poor, strangers and travelling Christians. The first missionaries travelled widely and were welcomed in a variety of homes (Acts 16:15, 32–34; 18:1–11), not just to make them feel at home, but to make it possible for them to carry on their ministry. Hospitality also included providing somewhere for believers to meet (Rom 16:3–5, 23; Col 4:15) when they came together for prayer, fellowship or to celebrate the Lord's Supper. It was a concrete way of expressing the respect and recognition called for in groups which were socio-economically and religiously diverse.

Hospitality, however, was not a mere practical expedient. After all, it didn't always work. Shared meals sometimes exposed tensions and inequalities in the church (Acts 10–11; 1 Cor 11:17–34; Gal 2:11–14; Jas 2:1–13). And it is not as if the church did not have other options. They could have gone for homogeneous churches (one for artisans, another for slaves, another for Jews, and so on). Or they could have abandoned the whole idea of the church as a community (which might have been difficult, since that is what the Greek word for 'church' means), and instead run a form of religious cinema, with people coming to enjoy the experience of worship or hear the preacher without bothering to relate to each other. The idea of bringing those of different classes and backgrounds together was just as alien then as it is now.

There was in fact a clear and irresistible theological warrant for hospitality. The notion of the incarnation with Jesus as a stranger on earth (cf. Luke 2:7, 4:16–30, 9:58; John 1:10–11), dependent on the generous support of others (cf. Luke 8:1–3, 9:1–6, 10:3–12, 38–42), made a permanent impression on early Christians. Not surprisingly, Matthew 25:31–46, Luke 14:12–14 and Hebrews 13:2 stress hospitality to strangers. The Greek word for 'hospitality' (cf. Rom 12:13; Heb 13:2; 1 Pet 4:9; 1 Tim 3:2; Titus 1:8) literally means 'love for the stranger'. Further, in the Gospels the presence of the kingdom is revealed in shared meals, such as in Luke 24:13–35, where Jesus turns the tables and appears not as guest but as host, and the disciples recognize him as their risen Lord. Paul urged believers to 'Welcome one another', as Christ had welcomed them (Rom 15:7).

The related responsibility, to show mercy in almsgiving (the Greek term for which is connected to the word for 'mercy') likewise had a profound theological basis. Such acts of compassion were to distinguish Christians as living advertisements of God's mercy in Christ. As those who have freely received, believers are freely to give. Charitable giving as the proper response to God's mercy was considered a mark of true spirituality. The ancient Jews taught that "almsgiving endures for ever" (Sirach 40:17b) and that God takes particular notice of our charitable deeds: "A man's almsgiving is like a signet with the Lord, and he will keep a person's kindness like the apple of his eye" (Sirach 17:22).

In Luke 11:41, almsgiving is valued more highly than matters of ritual purity, and in Luke 12:33 it is a mark of true discipleship. Such acts of mercy were highly regarded in the early church (Acts 9:36; 10:2) and were taken to be the regular obligation of Christians (cf. Acts 24:17). Generosity is a fruit of the Spirit (Gal 5:22, sometimes translated 'kindness'), and liberal giving is a gift of the Spirit (Rom 12:8). On the day of judgment, one thing the Son of Man will want to know is whether we have (unselfconsciously) carried out acts of mercy on behalf of those in need (Matt 25:31–46).

"It's enough for a man to understand his own business, and not to interfere with other people's. Mine occupies me constantly".[2] So growled Ebenezer Scrooge in Charles Dickens' *A Christmas Carol*, until, that is, he had been pardoned by 'the Spirits'. Following this life-changing experience, Scrooge gave up his odious, stingy, cold, unfeeling, tight-fisted, closed-hearted ways. Christians ought to be able to identify with Scrooge's transformation.

One example of a businessman who would have made an excellent role model for the new Scrooge (a name change might also have helped) is the founder of Hartley's (the jam-makers), Sir William Hartley (1846–1922). Hartley rose from humble origins to build a highly successful business which is still going today. He was known in his own day, however, far more for his amazing career of Christian philanthropy than for his impressive business acumen. At the age of twenty-nine he vowed to follow a course of systematic and proportionate giving, which held that as one's income grows, so should the percentage of money set aside for giving. In Hartley's opinion, "nothing raises money to a higher plane and gives it a higher interest than systematic giving. I sit on my money; I don't let it sit on me. To distribute my money is a harder and more anxious task than making it".[3]

Hartley did not find his commitment to giving easy, and he spoke often of the obstinacy of the selfish nature which we all share. His experience was that, in his own words, "the adoption of an enlightened policy is generally a gradual process, but the more we cultivate the spirit of Jesus Christ, the easier the thing becomes; and what appeared to us quite impossible at the beginning becomes not only possible but absolutely a joy".[4] Unlike the old Scrooge, Hartley regularly and voluntarily increased wages, practised profit-sharing and supplied low-cost, high-quality housing to some of his employees and free medical attention to all of them. He was also concerned for his suppliers, and would amend contracts in their favour if a change in the price of fruit and economic circumstances conspired against their making a decent living.

Taking up the collection

It normally takes just a minute or two in a church service for the obligatory offering. It might be collected during a hymn or it might be accompanied by awkward or embarrassed silence. Either way, to any outsider present it seems at best routine and at worst peripheral, or even irrelevant, to the worship. By contrast, Paul once took up a collection for the poor saints in Jerusalem that occupied much of his time and energy for more than five years (from the early 50s).

For whatever reason (perhaps a prolonged famine) the churches in Jerusalem were poor and badly in need of relief. Paul took for granted the solidarity of believers in Christ and called on the goodwill of the many churches in the east of the Roman Empire. It appears that this campaign for funds was a major focus of his second missionary journey. The gift was to symbolize the unity of both Jews and Gentiles in Christ (Rom 15:27). He regarded it as an act of fellowship (Rom 15:27, "share"), and compared it to a sacrificial offering (Rom 15:31, "my service for Jerusalem"; 2 Cor 8:20; 9:1, 12–13), an act of worship in and of itself. Whereas for us a cup of tea or coffee might symbolize Christian fellowship, Paul's idea of fellowship brought to mind a wallet or a cheque-book.

He treats the matter of the collection at length in 2 Corinthians 8–9, where the Corinthians are encouraged to finalize their contribution to the campaign. A number of principles for giving emerge from his appeal. Christians ought to share their possessions generously (8:2, 9:6, 13), enthusiastically (8:4, 11–12, 9:7), deliberately (9:7) and sensibly (8:11–15). They are to follow the supreme example of Christ, who gave up the wealth of his heavenly existence, becoming (materially) poor for the benefit of others, namely us, so that we might become (spiritually) rich (8:8–9). Paul also appeals to the example of the churches of Macedonia (8:1–5, 8), suggesting that as the world competes in getting rich, Christians ought to invert such aims and compete in being generous. And he endorses the principle of reciprocity, whereby fellow-believers supply each other's needs from their abundance, expecting nothing less in return should the situation some day be reversed (8:14).

Much of this seems to run up against the whole notion of privacy and confidentiality in giving. Didn't Jesus say, "when you give to the needy, do not let your left hand know what your right hand is doing" (Matt 6:3)? What business was it of the Corinthians to know that the Macedonians had given so handsomely? How can one Christian reciprocate the generosity of another unless both parties are in the know? And since a main form of giving was hospitality, wouldn't everyone notice which hands were serving the meals, hosting the meetings and supplying the lodgings?

It appears that we may have taken Jesus' instructions to an extreme and, in the process, diminished the essential collegiality and accountability of Christian giving. Many have turned Jesus' call to pure motives into an excuse to expect others to mind their own business. Jesus was concerned to combat that natural human tendency to ostentation and play-acting; he opposed the giving which is done in order to make ourselves look good in the eyes of others, which remains a real and powerful temptation. He did not, however, intend to drive the practice of giving underground, as is clear from the following verses, in which he counsels that to avoid the hypocrisy of praying to impress others we ought to pray alone in secret (Matt 6:5–6). Just as he had no intention of opposing all forms of corporate or group prayer, so also he did not wish to undercut the inevitable social dimension of giving and its essentially open and personal character.

The profile of an average Christian

In religion, as in sport and politics, groups define themselves not just by saying what they stand for and who they are, but also in terms of what they oppose and who they aren't. One group of supporters will insist not only that their team is known for its enterprising, attacking play, but also that their main rivals take a stifling, negative, defensive approach to the game. Political parties often stake their claim to being economically responsible or socially just by accusing the other parties of not living up to these ideals. The early Christians, as we pointed out in chapter 1, had no trouble in describing those who were outside their group: your average pagan worshipped idols, was sexually immoral and greedy. This was not so much a sober description of every individual who did not acknowledge Christ as Lord, as a way of asserting the core values of their own group.

If a local church today were asked to draw up a profile of your average Christian, I wonder what it would look like. It might refer to matters of piety like Bible reading, prayer and church attendance. When Aristides, the converted Athenian Greek philosopher, attempted to characterize the Christians around AD 150, it was to the positive counterparts to idolatry, sexual immorality and greed that he pointed. First, Christians are those who "worship no other God than him ... God the Creator and Maker of all things ... They do not worship strange gods". Furthermore, "their wives ... are pure as virgins and their daughters modest, and their men refrain from all unlawful intercourse and all uncleanness". And finally, "if they see a stranger, they bring him under their roof ... if they hear that any of their number is imprisoned or oppressed ... all of them provide for his needs ... And if there is among them a man that is poor and needy ... they fast two or three days that they may supply the needy with the necessary food".[5]

In the early church, the sharing of possessions was thus just as central to what it means to be a Christian, as are the exclusive worship of the true God and the matter of sexual purity. Christians in the first or second century would have been just as perplexed to find a confessing Christian who worshipped idols, or was openly adulterous, as they would have been to meet one who refused to share his or her possessions. Paul thought giving so basic that he enjoined the former thief to:

> *labour, doing honest work with his own hands, [not so that he can look after himself, but] so that he may have something to share with anyone in need* (EPH 4:28).

Whereas our first concern for those out of work is that they may find a job in order to become self-supporting, Paul's was that they might be in a position to support others.

Rather than seeing themselves as individuals who happened to be Christians, the earliest Christians regarded themselves in the first place as members of the body of Christ, and took for granted their obligations to support one another, materially when necessary. Whatever might be said about the appropriate channels and methods of giving today, it should not escape our notice how far we have drifted from this point of view. A rich Christian may not be a contradiction in terms, but a mean and greedy Christian certainly is.

ENDNOTES
1. *On the Death of Peregrinus* 1.
2. Charles Dickens, *A Christmas Carol* (1843; Oxford: OUP, 1988), p. 12.
3. Arthur S. Peake, *The Life of Sir William Hartley* (London: Hodder and Stoughton, 1926), p. 76.
4. Peake, *The Life of Sir William Hartley*, p. 78.
5. Aristides, *Apology* 15.1–10.

HOW TO HAVE A FINANCIAL MELTDOWN
Peter Hastie[*]

Oliver Cromwell, the Lord Protector of England, was faced with a financial crisis. His government had run out of silver, and could no longer mint coins. A man of great resourcefulness, he sent his Treasurer on a mission to see if he could find more of the precious metal. When the Treasurer returned, he reported that the only silver he could find was in the statues of the saints, which were kept in various cathedrals around the country.

"Good!" Cromwell said with glee, "We'll melt down the saints and put them into circulation".

While Cromwell's approach to a monetary crisis would certainly raise the eyebrows of today's economists, he stated a vital principle which would solve most of the funding problems of our Church. For Cromwell, the difficulty was not a lack of silver. There was plenty of the precious metal around. The difficulty was that it was contained in the saints, and was not easily accessible.

We face the same problem. The Lord has put plenty of money in the pockets of Christians. It's just that sometimes it's not particularly accessible for the work of the Kingdom. The question is: "How do we melt down the saints and put their wealth to work for Christ?"

This is a crucial matter for the Church because so much turns on it. It's not just that certain ministries flounder because we run out of funds. That's bad enough, especially if the ministry is worthwhile. What is even more important is that our lack of generosity is fatal to our spiritual development. I suspect that this is something that we've hardly considered.

That's why the New Testament's plan for "melting down the saints and putting them into circulation" is one that should grip

---

[*] Originally published in *The Briefing*, #82/83 and 84.

our attention. The Apostle Paul seemed to have a view on most things, and church finances and giving was certainly one of them. He always brings the force of eternal principles to bear on the most mundane matters, including the issue of money.

The occasion on which Paul dealt exhaustively with this issue was during his fund-raising tour of Greece in aid of the impoverished Church in Jerusalem. Paul's approach to the raising of funds is quite novel, and stands in marked contrast to many of the modern techniques that are used in our churches.

The first thing that strikes us about Paul's view of fund-raising is that he describes our donations as a 'grace' or 'gift' which God has given to us. In 2 Corinthians 8 he uses the term 'gift' or 'grace' four times to refer to the giving of the churches in Macedonia and Corinth (2 Cor 8:4, 6, 7). This means that the opportunity for us to give, and even the inclination to do so, are spiritual gifts. I sometimes wonder how many of us think that appeals for service or money are troublesome burdens, or even worse, a painful tax. If that's how we view giving, it seems to me that we are not in the same league as Paul. He says that the desire and opportunity to give is actually a spiritual gift or 'grace' from God. If this is so, then we should be thankful for every opportunity to give to God, because we'll see each occasion as a gift.

One of our major difficulties is that we have not grasped that the act of giving is a spiritual grace. When many of us think of spiritual gifts, we tend to concentrate, like the Corinthians, on the more exotic gifts like tongues, healing and prophecy. We forget that giving is a grace that is given by God himself, and represents the high-water mark of the Christian life. Why? Because it's the gift of God's own nature to us. We can have the gifts of tongues, or prophecy, but have none of God's likeness. However, it's impossible to have the 'grace of giving' without reflecting the love of God. And it's the presence of God's love in our souls that is the mark of spiritual maturity.

That's why the money problem in our churches is never really financial. It's a spiritual problem. It's a question of whether we have grace; we are only complete as this grace of generosity shines out of us. The Christian life is like an expensive diamond ring, with a large diamond in the centre of a cluster of smaller diamonds. Generosity is the large diamond. The other gifts form the cluster.

Now since Christian generosity is a gift, it's not something that a church or preacher can command (vv 8, 10). While Paul spoke openly about money, he only offered advice and counsel. He never coerced anyone. He never tried to enslave people to a system of giving, or forced them to feel some sense of personal obligation to himself. When he spoke about the giving of the Macedonian church there was not even the slightest hint that the collection had been forced upon them as a duty or as an ecclesiastical tax of 10%. We search in vain for such ideas. Modern church fund-raisers might resort to these notions, but not Paul. And the reason why is that Christian generosity is a spiritual gift from God which cannot be commanded.

Naturally, this raises the question: "If New Testament giving cannot be understood as a tax, but is rather a God-given opportunity to become like Christ, how do we determine the amount we should give?"

Personal Divestment—A Guide to Christian Giving

I remember sitting in a church in Melbourne some years ago and listening to the treasurer explain a new system of giving that the deacons wanted to introduce. We were each handed a scale of incomes beginning with the old age pension and gradually increasing to senior executive rates. Against each level of income was an amount that we were expected to give. It worked out at 10%. The deacons could have saved themselves some paper. We had no trouble moving the decimal point for ourselves. But it set me thinking: "What should I give for the Lord's work? Was 10% the standard?"

According to the treasurer, 10% was the law of heaven. But I wanted to be sure.

So I began to search the New Testament for an answer, and struck gold in Paul's second letter to the Corinthians. I didn't know why I hadn't thought of it before, but Paul's answer to the question "How much?" was simple: imitate Christ. To the question of "How much?", Paul said:

> ... *you know the grace of our Lord Jesus Christ, that though he was rich, yet for your sake he became poor, so that you by his poverty might become rich* (2 COR 8:9).

It's strange how you can overlook the obvious, isn't it? Perhaps the notion of a flat 10% was so deeply ingrained in me that I never even considered the possibility of another standard. But there it was, as plain as day. No mention of a tithe—just an invitation to imitate Christ.

I find it interesting that Paul always seems to refer questions of faith and conduct back to Jesus Christ and the gospel. He loves to remind us that Jesus is the Christian's model. But it was at this point that I struck a problem. As I searched the Gospels, I couldn't find any instance of Jesus making a contribution to the church of his day—apart from his payment of the temple tax. And this tax could hardly be the standard for my giving. The ordinary Jew gave far more than that.

However, although Paul didn't provide me with an indication of how much Jesus gave for the support of his synagogue, nevertheless he came up with a helpful rule of thumb. In seeking to imitate Christ, it's not the acts of Jesus so much as the spirit of Jesus that is all-important. When Paul pleaded with the Corinthians to be generous with their money, he reminded them of the generosity of Christ, who forsook his glory and became poor for us. One action involved money; the other was related to the surrender of a life. But the spirit of both acts was the same. All Paul is saying is that it's the mind of Christ that's crucial in this matter of giving.

So we come back to the original question: "How much do I give?" The answer is simple: "What did Jesus give?" Paul says:

... though he was rich, yet for your sake he became poor ...

At one time, Jesus possessed the combined wealth of heaven and earth. It was his alone at creation. But then something strange happened. The infinite God became an infant boy. The Son of God abandoned the glory of an eternal throne for the squalor of a stable floor. He became utterly destitute. Had Jesus given only 10%, he would still have ranked in the Forbes Top 100. But he gave far more than the tithe. He gave to the point of total self-denial. There was nothing calculated or measured about his sacrifice. He gave freely. And that, says Paul, is the measure of Christian giving.

For some of us, that will mean that we can't give 10%. A tithe may push some Christians below the poverty line. But for others with substantial incomes, we can afford to give much more than a tithe. John Wesley followed a sensible policy. Out of his yearly stipend, he lived on £28 and gave the remaining £2 to the Lord. The following year his salary doubled, but he found that he could still live comfortably on the £28, and so instead of raising his standard of living, he resolved to give away the greater part of his increase to the Lord. Wesley had the mind of Christ.

The challenge before us is to think like Jesus. Out of his deep love for us, Jesus gave away his very life. Paul challenges us to do the same. And as we meditate on the grace of Christ, we'll give our lives to him.

FAITH AND WORKS; RICH AND POOR
John Dickson[*]

*What good is it, my brothers, if someone says he has faith but
does not have works? Can that faith save him? If a brother or
sister is poorly clothed and lacking in daily food, and one of
you says to them, "Go in peace, be warmed and filled", without
giving them the things needed for the body, what good is that?
So also faith by itself, if it does not have works, is dead. But
someone will say, "You have faith and I have works". Show me
your faith apart from your works, and I will show you my faith
by my works. You believe that God is one; you do well. Even
the demons believe—and shudder! Do you want to be shown,
you foolish person, that faith apart from works is useless?
Was not Abraham our father justified by works when he offered
up his son Isaac on the altar? You see that faith was active
along with his works, and faith was completed by his works;
and the Scripture was fulfilled that says, "Abraham believed
God, and it was counted to him as righteousness"—and he was
called a friend of God. You see that a person is justified by
works and not by faith alone. And in the same way was not
also Rahab the prostitute justified by works when she received
the messengers and sent them out by another way? For as the
body apart from the spirit is dead, so also faith apart from
works is dead* (JAMES 2:14-26).

Introduction
1. The controversy of James chapter 2
James 2:14-26 is one of the most controversial passages in the book
of James. In fact, in some theological circles the passage has been
regarded as the most problematic portion of the entire New Testament.

[*] Previously unpublished sermon.

The 16th century Reformer, Martin Luther—the man most responsible for the birth of the Protestant church—described the letter of James, on the basis of our text, as *ein rechte stroern Epistel* ("a right epistle of straw"). In the famous Luther Bible, published throughout Europe in 1522, Luther arranged to have James placed at the back without a page number reference in the table of contents.

In short, Luther believed the Epistle of James was inconsistent with the doctrine of justification by faith, a doctrine he had rightly brought to the centre of his theological discourse. Whereas Paul affirmed, "For by grace you have been saved through faith. And this is not your own doing; it is the gift of God, not a result of works, so that no one may boast" (Eph 2:8-9), James insisted, "a person is justified by works and not by faith alone". What further evidence was required, thought Luther: James had to go.

It fell to a later 16th-century reformer, John Calvin, to try to resolve the tension perceived by Luther between Paul and James and between faith and works. Calvin argued that a 'faith' which does not issue forth in good works is not true faith. It is merely a kind of assent to a series of propositions. True faith, said Calvin, is a trust in the promises of God which submits to his word and, by the power of the Holy Spirit, moves the believer to a life of holiness. The point is beautifully put in a famous quotation attributed to Calvin (but as yet un-sourced by this author): "We are justified by faith alone, but the faith which justifies is never alone".

In this simple statement the teaching of James and the teaching of Paul may be reconciled. James addresses not nervous Gentiles who fear that justification comes through performing the works of the Law (Paul's audience), but presumptuous Jews who suppose that justification comes on the basis of mere assent to God and his Messiah, and that devotion to the Messiah's law of love is optional.

2. Is James chapter 2 a 'theology' of faith and works?

However, this Calvinist resolution of the perceived tension between Paul and James and between faith and works has not stopped James 2:14-26 remaining a 'controversial' passage for modern Bible commentators and preachers. Open any commentary, or listen to any sermon, on this passage and you will find that a bulk of the discussion is devoted to reconciling Paul and James or, at the very least, theologizing about the connection between faith and works.

Such discussions, of course, have their place. However, it is the argument of this paper that in seeking to bring our important Reformation insights to bear on the text of James we may have missed the rhetorical point of this important passage of Scripture.

James 2:14-26 was never designed to make merely a theological point, as if James were worried about his audience's purity of doctrine. What theology there is in chapter two has a practical intention. It is designed to get James' beloved readers doing something they were neglecting, something that was fundamental to Christian faith as James saw it, something without which one ought not even *claim* to have true faith.

The discussion of James 2:14-26 is intended to redress the perverse scenario narrated in verses 15 and 16:

> *If a brother or sister is poorly clothed and lacking in daily food,*
> *and one of you says to them, "Go in peace, be warmed and*
> *filled," without giving them the things needed for the body,*
> *what good is that?*

The scenario described in these verses is not merely a kind of sermon illustration designed to highlight a larger theological point about the connection between faith and works (such an 'illustration' is offered in the examples of Abraham and Rahab in 2:21-25). It is in fact the reason for the entire discussion: Christians had been ignoring the plight of the poor.

Attention to the context shows that James has been building up to this point, with hint and innuendo, ever since chapter 1:27.

The context of 2:15-16

1. The 'religion' God approves (1:27)

In what is the climactic statement of the introduction to the epistle, James flags a theme that sounds foreign to modern ears but was central to early Christianity: true religion attends to the needs of the destitute. "Religion that is pure and undefiled before God, the Father, is this: to visit orphans and widows in their affliction, and to keep oneself unstained from the world" (James 1:27).

Orphans and widows were the archetypal poor people in the ancient world. They had few rights, very little power, no status and, without any social welfare system in antiquity, they were almost always utterly impoverished. Pure religion, however, says James, redresses that: it 'looks after' orphans and widows in their distress.

Within months of the birth of the early church a daily distribution system was set up for widows and other destitute persons. We catch a glimpse of it in Acts 6:

Now in these days when the disciples were increasing in
number, a complaint by the Hellenists arose against the
Hebrews because their widows were being neglected in the daily
distribution (Acts 6:1).

This was common practice throughout early Christianity. In fact, we know that the church of the city of Rome, in the middle of the 200's, supported daily more than 1500 widows, orphans and impoverished persons (*Eccl. Hist.* 6.43.11). Specialist ministers were employed by the church to oversee the task.

Pure religion, says James, also involves keeping "oneself from being polluted by the world". Make no mistake, this has little to do with the sex, drugs and rock-and-roll kind of worldly pollution. It is entirely to do with avoiding the perverse socio-economic attitudes of ancient society. James goes on in the very next sentence to attack an aspect of that worldly pollution in the form of favouritism to the rich at the expense of the poor:

> *My brothers, show no partiality as you hold the faith in our*
> *Lord Jesus Christ, the Lord of glory. For if a man wearing a*
> *gold ring and fine clothing comes into your assembly, and a*
> *poor man in shabby clothing also comes in ...* (JAMES 2:1-2).

To "keep oneself from being polluted by the world" means to spurn society's usual treatment of rich and poor.

This observation reveals a very neat structure to the teaching of chapter two. The final statement of the introduction to the letter (1:27), states in antithetical form the essential character of pure religion: it cares for the *poor* of the world and shuns the (economic) *perversions* of the world. Chapter two then immediately unpacks this twofold-theme, in reverse order: verses 1-13 call for an end to worldly favouritism, then verses 14-26 call for charity toward the poor.

2. True mercy (2:13): transition statement

In between these two sections (2:1-3 and 14-26) is another reminder of James' financial, rather than merely theological, concerns throughout chapter two: "For judgment is without mercy to one who has shown no mercy. Mercy triumphs over judgment" (v. 13). This text is often treated as the conclusion to the issue of favouritism, but it is more accurate to view the verse as the clever transition from one section to another: it concludes the teaching about our treatment of the rich and introduces the teaching about our treatment of the poor.

Key to this transition is the meaning of the word 'merciful'. In our tradition, we tend to think of 'mercy' almost exclusively in terms of 'divine pardon'. When used of God, that is usually what the term *does* mean. But when used of *human* behaviour, 'mercy' usually means something like 'charity/generosity'. In fact, the central Old and New Testament expression for what we would call 'charitable giving' is literally the phrase 'to have mercy' (Matt 6:2, 3, 4; Luke 11:41; 12:33; Acts 3:2, 3, 10; 9:36; 10:2, 4, 31; 24:17).

The thought is captured well in Jesus' most famous parable, the parable of the Good Samaritan. You may remember that the parable is an explanation to a Jewish leader of what it means to 'love your neighbour as yourself'. After contrasting the stingy actions of the priest and Levite with the generous charity of the Samaritan, Jesus concludes:

> Which of these three, do you think, proved to be a neighbour to the man who fell among the robbers?" He said, "The one who showed him mercy". And Jesus said to him, "You go, and do likewise" (LUKE 10:36-37).

This is the idea of 'mercy' which stands behind James' teaching in chapter 2. Shaming the poor in favour of the rich is to withhold mercy and will result, says James, in God withholding his mercy from us at the judgement. When James says judgement without mercy will be shown to anyone who has not been *merciful*, he means that being merciful to the poor is so basic to Christian faith that those who have not displayed such mercy prove themselves never to have known the kindness, or mercy, of God.

It is the perfect introduction to the words which immediately follow.

The scenario of 2:15-16

It should be clear by now that James' concern in the passage is not to offer his readers a correct understanding of the theological relationship between faith and works, as important as that is. It is rather to highlight their fundamental betrayal of true faith, or 'pure religion', in not caring for the destitute.

1. Sentiment toward the poor

James does concede that the hypothetical Christian in his scenario possesses a certain sentimental feeling toward the poor: "Go in peace [says the church member to the poor]; be warm and filled"

(2:16). The believer here does at least *hope* for the comfort of the poor; it's not as if there's no concern at all.

The words translated "Go in peace" imply a *spiritual* sentiment as well. It recalls the traditional Jewish and Christian departure blessing: May God's peace be upon you. Modern Jews still say it: 'shalom'.

2. Meeting the needs of the poor

The problem is that the 'religion' which God accepts as 'pure and faultless'—'true faith' in other words—is not a mere sentiment. If a Christian does nothing about the physical needs of the impoverished, says James in verse 16, his or her sentiment is no 'good'. Worse, in the words of verse 17: So also [literally: 'in *this* way'], faith by itself, if it does not have works, is dead". James is at least saying that a Christian who *blesses* the poor but doesn't *provide* for the poor is not doing well in the faith.

Lest this article leave readers merely with a *sentiment* toward the poor, let me offer some modern reflections.

Poverty today

1. World poverty and government assistance

Did you know that a billion people in the world right now live on less than a dollar a day? That's not a US dollar spent in a third-world country. It's a dollar as calculated by a World Bank system known as Purchasing Power Parity (PPP), which measures "the relative purchasing power of currencies across countries". Broadly speaking, that means that if you can imagine what living in Australia on less than a dollar a day would feel like, you can imagine the plight of one billion people throughout the world, many of whom are your brothers and sisters in Christ.

And did you know what percentage of Australia's Gross National Income (GNI) is spent on Overseas Aid and Development

(OAD)? One quarter of one percent (0.25%. Source: OECD website) and falling. And while Australia does better than some in the OECD, notably the US, we are worse than a lot of those 30 nations, including New Zealand, the UK, France, and Ireland. Denmark, for instance, quadruples our percentage figure.

It is important to realize that we must not rely on our taxes to redress world poverty. The reality is that the amount is miniscule. If a household is paying, say, $50,000 tax a year, only $125 of that is going to relieve the world's poor.

2. Australian spending patterns (the ABS figures)

And while we're on the topic of household spending, it is worth mentioning what the average Australian household—not individual—spends on all forms of charitable giving in a year. It is a total of $267 per household, or just over half a percent (0.58%. Source: ABS Household Expenditure Survey, Sept 2000) of the average income.

Households in the upper 20 percent income range—that's households earning $100,000 before tax—spend, on average, $344 a year on charitable giving. That's a *third* of one percent (0.33%) of income: the wealthier, the less generous!

Figures can be numbing, but just consider the household expenditure (of the upper 20% quintile) on other items: we spend more on our pets each year ($445.12) than we do on charity ($344); we spend almost *twice* as much on confectionary ($627.64); more than *four* times as much on beer and wine ($1,488.76); nearly *ten* times as much on restaurant and take-away meals ($3,329.04).

Many readers will be more generous than these ABS figures indicate. But it is still worth asking: would you give as much to relieve poverty as you would spend on, say, your DVD or shoe collection, or your wine cellar, or your holidays, or sporting events? And if not, why not? What possible reason could there be for not matching one's luxuries with generosity to the destitute?

Of course, no-one is advocating giving *everything* away. And, clearly, there is no suggestion that being wealthy is in any way unchristian. But in the Scriptures, the rich are urged to *match* their wealth with *generosity*. What else could loving your neighbour as yourself mean in monetary terms? Consider this statement by the apostle Paul (with which James would surely have agreed):

> As for the rich in this present age, charge them not to be haughty, nor to set their hopes on the uncertainty of riches, but on God, who richly provides us with everything to enjoy. They are to do good, to be rich in good works, to be generous and ready to share (1 TIM 6:17-18).

This is what the apostle asked to be commanded to the rich. The rich (that is most of Western Christendom) are to put their hope in God, and match their wealth by being rich in good works, especially good works of a financial type—being generous and willing to share.

3. A simple equation

On the assumption that wealth should be matched with generosity, let me close by proposing a simple, practical equation. It is not a rule to beat yourself over the head with; just a guideline to liberate your use of money.

Why not be as *generous* to others as you are *luxurious* with yourself?

Don't feel guilty about buying a nice bottle of wine. Just match it with a gift to Anglicare. By all means, get take-away when you've had a tough day and can't be bothered cooking, but why not send the same amount to TEAR Fund, Opportunity International or World Vision, three of the world's most highly regarded, and coincidentally Christian, aid organizations.

It's fantastic that the Lord has blessed us with the resources to frequent sporting events, the movies, the golf course, restaurants and the theatre, but why on earth would we not budget, with equal liberality, to put food in the mouth and clothes on the back of the world's impoverished. Why not be as *generous* to others as you are *luxurious* with yourself?

May it never be said of us that we merely have a sentiment toward the poor but do nothing about it. For, as James insists, "faith apart from works is dead".

A CHRISTIAN LIFESTYLE

THE CHRISTIAN AND MONEY
D. B. Knox[*]

Money figures largely in our thoughts. We occupy a lot of time thinking about it, about how much we have got, how much we need, how much we earn, how much we spend. The New Testament also has a lot to say about money, and what it says is quite remarkable because it is the opposite to what we normally think about money.

Before we examine what the New Testament says about it we need to ask ourselves whether we are willing to accept God's thoughts on the subject of money when these are clearly announced in the pages of the Bible and particularly taught by Jesus himself. Does God the Creator know more about the management of money than we do, and are we willing to accept his words as the rule for our conduct in this subject to which we give so much of our attention? Christian obedience means complete obedience and not only in those things where we happen to agree with God. Christian faith means trusting God even when our own views seem to suggest the contrary.

The first thing to note in the Bible teaching about money is that affluence is unimportant. Having a little more or a little less is irrelevant to life. Jesus taught this very clearly when he said, "A man's life does not consist in the abundance of his possessions" (Luke 12:15). From this it follows that the first virtue to be cultivated with regard to the handling of money is the virtue of contentment. Thus, Paul teaches clearly that having food and clothing, with these we should be content (1 Tim 6:8). His remarks are in the context of his condemnation of Christians who think that the Christian life, and particularly the Christian ministry, is a way of making money and becoming rich, and he comments, "the Christian life with contentment is great riches". Godliness with contentment—that is the

* Originally published in *The Briefing*, #251.

apostle's recipe for living, and what wonderful peace it brings, complete release from the rat-race. We are to live within our circumstances, for our circumstances are God-given. God is sovereign. The silver and gold are his. He is able to multiply money if we need it as easily as he multiplied the loaves and fishes on the hillside in Galilee, or as he multiplies the grain by turning it into the ear of corn through his rain and his sunshine and the fertile soil of his creation. If we look after God's affairs, he will look after us.

The second point about money that the Bible underlines is an obvious one, namely that affluence is unreliable. We can lose it quickly, and we all lose it at all events at death or in old age when it is no use to us (as we are too weak to do anything with it). Jesus, therefore, warned his disciples not to be rich in this world but rather to be rich in the next, rich towards God. He told the story of the rich farmer whose fields had produced abundant harvests. Instead of thanking God he simply said, "I will do this: I will tear down my barns and build larger ones, and there I will store all my grain and my goods. And I will say to my soul, Soul, you have ample goods laid up for many years; relax, eat, drink, be merry." But God said to him, "Fool! This night your soul is required of you, and the things you have prepared, whose will they be?" And Jesus added, "So is the one who lays up treasure for himself and is not rich toward God" (Luke 12:18-21). Money tempts us very strongly to put our trust in it, but it is a very uncertain thing, and after all is completely under God's control. Thus, the apostle tells Timothy, "As for the rich in this present age, charge them not to be haughty, not to set their hopes on the uncertainty of riches, but on God, who richly provides us with everything to enjoy" (1 Tim 6:17). They are to do good, to be rich in good deeds, liberal and generous, thus laying up for themselves a good foundation for the future, so that they may take hold of the life which is life indeed.

Affluence is unreliable. It is a snare to rely on money for the future. Our trust must be in God, who is in charge of our future and who will supply our needs, because he cares for us.

II

In considering the Christian use of money it is important to realize that we must act responsibly in the use of the money under our control. The first principle that we may mention is that we must be willing to share our money with those in real need whom God's providence brings within the orbit of our life. It is not as though we have to go without in order that others might have affluence, but rather that we might share our blessings with those who have need of our help.

There are two great obstacles to sharing. The first is greed. We want more and more for ourselves. Greed is self-centred, and can only be cured by God. We must call upon him in prayer to give us his Holy Spirit so that our attitudes to life may agree with his character. God himself is a giving God. He gives us everything to enjoy fully. He has given us his Son to be our saviour. When we love God we will be able to love our brother, so we will rise above greedy and selfish use of our money and share our resources with those who have real need. Greediness grows if encouraged—we may be surprised how greedy we have become without noticing it. Of course, gambling is essentially greed, and an individual or a community that indulges in gambling (and it doesn't matter how small the sum), will become more and more greedy, and therefore less and less inclined to help one another in times of need. Gambling has this effect even if the sum is small because its motive is just as much greed as if the sum is large. It is sad that the Government is encouraging this vice of greed in order to obtain taxes. For it will undoubtedly have an evil effect on community and community response in times of crisis. Moreover, the greedy person is not a happy person. He is never satisfied with his self-centredness.

The other obstacle to sharing our money is fear. We are frightened that we will leave ourselves short if we give it away; not short perhaps in the present, because we can estimate that, but in the future with all its uncertainties. The answer to this sort of fear is faith in God's faithfulness in the future. It is he who has given us our present possessions and he has promised that, if we seek to do his will, he will give to us what we need when we need it. God is in control of every event in our world, including the business world, and the world of our own private life. He has promised us heaven and a wonderful heavenly inheritance, and Christians should live in the light of that promise. He has promised provision for the rest of life that is this side of heaven, and we should live in the light of this promise as well. So when you are tempted to hesitate in helping other people in their real need as you come across the need, remember God's promise to be faithful. He who has given us life will give us the means to sustain life and not only our life, but the life of our children too. Indeed, as St Paul says, the love of God is such that we have no grounds for fear. He wrote, "He who did not spare his own Son but gave him up for us all, how will he not also with him graciously give us all things?" (Rom 8:32). We have a great inheritance in the future. Christ has provided it through his death, and we have already begun to enjoy it through his Spirit. If we keep our thoughts on this inheritance, we won't clutch to ourselves what God has given us in this life, but will share it with generosity. Sharing is the first great principle in the use of our money.

III

In considering the Christian's use of his money, another principle to be remembered is that no-one, whether Christian or non-Christian, should ever have as a primary aim, the aim to make money. This is because such an aim, when it is the primary aim, is self-centred and we should never be self-centred in our actions towards others. The use of money, whether in business or in any other way, brings us into contact with people, and all our contacts and relationships with other people should be with the object of serving them. This is the principle on which human life has been made by God. This is the principle exemplified by Jesus Christ, the Son of God "who is among you as one who serves". If we aim primarily at making money when we are in contact with other people, we aim at something selfish; we are looking to our own self interests rather than the interests of those with whom we are in contact, and this remains true whether we expand the concept of self into self and family, or into religious objectives in which we are interested.

Consequently, in our use of money, whether we are conducting a business or developing a property or investing in shares, our primary aim and motive must never be to make money but rather to see how we can serve other people with the money God has put in our control. This applies to all people but especially, of course, to Christians and the Christian church.

For example, if we have a block of land which we wish to develop, it must not be primarily to make money from it; but we must ask ourselves whether through the development we are serving the community. Similarly, if we are landlords, we must, in conducting our business with our tenants, not primarily aim to make money out of them but rather to serve them, since we have been put by providence into this position of serving them as landlords. We are not to get rid of our tenants because we find serving their interests inconvenient. If we are businessmen, our business must be conducted to confer benefit on our customers, and similarly directors of public companies must not be primarily interested in the size of the profit which they are able to announce in their annual report to the shareholders, but they must be primarily concerned with the people their company comes into contact with through its business. All this does not mean that we are not to make money. Of course we need to make a profit if we are going to maintain our home and family, and if we are going to have money to invest for the better development of community resources; but the primary aim and motivation of our actions when we are in relation to other people must not be to make money but rather to serve those other people within the parameters that the need to maintain the service, through having enough to live on and develop our resources, requires. In a word, no-one, Christian or non-

Christian, in using his money, should have as his primary aim the making of money, or even the conserving of his equity, but his aim should always be that which Jesus had, namely true concern and service for his neighbour.

The money under our control, or the property which we own, is simply that part of God's creation which we have the responsibility for using. And we must use it in accordance with the character of God, its creator. Our using it will bring us into contact with people. This means that we must serve them in our using it, for serving other people is the true motive for actions in our relations with other people.

NOT KEEPING UP WITH THE JONESES: THE CHRISTIAN PRACTICE OF BECOMING POORER

Sandra King[*]

Few people enjoy being poor. Even fewer people choose it. Many people in the world are born to it. And while we Christians may not seek poverty, in a material sense, following Jesus is costly and may require us to become poorer.

Consider a French friend of mine, Marc, who was recently fired from his job. He worked for a small company. One day his boss offered to take him out for lunch (a bad sign) and it was there that his boss explained that he would have to 'let him go', not because of any fault in his work, but because the boss's wife didn't like Marc. Now under French law, Marc would be perfectly entitled to sue his boss for wrongful dismissal and he would most likely have won. But Marc explained to his boss that he wouldn't be suing, that he was sorry it hadn't worked out, that he was a Christian and that he trusted God for his future. The boss wanted to know more about Jesus, and Marc presented the gospel. Now both Marc and his wife are unemployed (she has been looking for work for a while) in a country with over 10% unemployment. But the gospel convicted Marc not to pursue his former employer in the courts, and he is now the poorer for it.

Consider stories that we have heard in years past from former communist countries, where being known as a Christian meant a loss of entitlement to work. Who provided for the families of such faithful followers of Christ? The cost was great, not least being financial ruin. We have perhaps met the Christians in business who, by refusing to work longer and longer hours because they had commitments to their family or church, lost their jobs or were moved sideways. Or those who couldn't agree with dishonest busi-

* Originally published in *The Briefing*, #251.

ness practices. Or the woman who resigned from her job because she could no longer put up with the sexual advances of a colleague.

All these are examples of Christians who, wanting to follow Jesus, made difficult and costly choices that made them materially poorer. I would like to commend to us another way of becoming poorer for the sake of the Gospel: giving away our wealth, freely and cheerfully and at great cost.

In 2 Corinthians 8 and 9 we have the outstanding example of the Macedonian Christians:

> ... for in a severe test of affliction, their abundance of joy and their extreme poverty have overflowed in a wealth of generosity on their part. For they gave according to their means, as I can testify, and beyond their means ... (2 COR 8:2-3).

These Christians longed to give, that they might aid their Christian brothers in need. They gave eagerly. They gave in their poverty. They gave more than they could afford, such was their desire (8:3-4). Such generosity is honouring to God (9:13).

Such radical generosity should challenge us. The Macedonian Christians gave in their poverty and more than they could afford. We are not told what practical implications this had for them, but we can perhaps imagine. There was less money in the family budget. How did they explain to their children that there would be less food in the house for a while but that Christians elsewhere urgently needed the money? What did the neighbours say? Such poor management of funds. Such an unwise decision. What of the future? What about the approaching wedding in the family? No more reading lessons for a while. What the Macedonians did was unreasonable and very short sighted—in fact, downright irresponsible!

The Bible describes the generosity of the Macedonian Christians as being a result of the grace of God. In fact, Paul writes in such a way as to ask the Christians in Corinth, who were probably wealthier, to outdo the Macedonians in generosity. We Christians rarely try to outdo each other in our generosity. More often than not, we seek to outdo each other by succeeding in the non-Christian society around us.

While we may be disapproving of our society which clamours after the god of Money and all the power that Money gives, can we Christians see any difference between ourselves and our unbelieving neighbour? Do we have the same number of cars? Do we have the same quality of clothing? Do our children have the same number of music classes? Do we have the same level of superannuation? Are we as demanding in our quality of life—our health care, our vacation destinations, our entertainment? Do we desire the same amount of space in our home, the same conveniences, the same number of CDs?

In short, in what ways have we Christians decided to deny ourselves because we do not follow the god of Money?

Imagine this conversation between two work colleagues:

Joe: You'll never believe what I saw this morning!

Peter: What was that?

Joe: I saw our General Manager catching the bus to work and last week, too. What gives? Aren't the profits rolling in this year? I mean a bus! Why not a car or a taxi?

Peter: He's a Christian.

Joe: Ohhh. (This is a very knowing oh. Like 'Oh now I get it'.) There is a momentary pause.

Joe: What do Christians do with their money? I mean our boss must be earning heaps. And you know that judge who has been on TV?

Peter: Yeah.

Joe: Well he's a Christian too. I know because he lives in my suburb. He must earn megabucks, but you couldn't tell by his house. What do they do with their money?

Peter: I hear that they give it away.

How are we Christians going to live in a money-loving world and yet not be of this world? How are we to put to death whatever belongs to our earthly nature: sexual immorality, impurity, lust, evil desires and greed, which is idolatry (Col 3:5,6). How are we going to resist serving the god of Money? Following are some suggestions, some biblical, some practical.

1. Contentment

Keep your life free from love of money, and be content with what you have, for [God] has said, "I will never leave you nor forsake you" (HEB 13: 5).

Now there is great gain in godliness with contentment (1 TIM 6:6).

Contentment is something to pray for and to learn (Phil 4:11). Instead of letting our eyes glance longingly towards what our neighbour has (and why do we only ever compare ourselves with our wealthy neighbour and not our poor neighbour?), we should set our eyes on the Kingdom of God. Instead of setting our hearts on treasures that rust and rot, we should set our hearts on the treasures of heaven (Matt 6:19-21).

2. Do not steal

To steal is to take what we want with a disregard for the law of God. It is to choose to take what Money offers instead of obeying Christ. As difficult as it may be, we must resist the temptation to take what is not ours: money from the government; computer software copied illegally; money duly owed to musicians through the sale of CDs. All this may seem tedious, but our allegiance is to Christ who calls us to steal no longer but to work, doing something useful with our hands (Eph 4:28).

3. Give, give, give

How can we serve something that we give away? Here is a sure cure to materialism: give it away. After commanding us to steal no more, God tells us to "labour ... that [we] may have something to share with anyone in need" (Eph 4:28). Each time we give, we remind ourselves that we do not live for Money, nor for its power. What we have is from God and we are his agents to be generous and to share with those in need.

4. Include the children

Our reaction is often this: I don't mind paying the cost of following Christ, but I can't really impose that on my kids. I will do without, but my kids shouldn't be deprived. Following Jesus involves the cost of our lives, but we know that we wouldn't live any other way. Jesus' way is the best way for me and for my children. If following Christ means having treasures other than the passing earthly things that Money offers, then we want our children to learn this with us. As parents, we have the wonderful opportunity of modelling to our children cheerful generosity, and of supporting them as they come into contact with the non-Christian society that will tempt them to abandon Christ. How will our children learn about the costs and joys of following Christ if we don't help them live it while they are in our care?

Consider this scene. What ending do you find the most acceptable?

Look kids. Your mum and I have been doing some thinking and praying about our holidays. We've decided that we won't be going away this year. I'm really sorry, but:

(a) since I've lost my job we are just going to have to cut down on our activities. When I find a new job, we'll reconsider things.

(b) we've decided to buy a house and for the next year or so we are all going to have to pull in our belts so we can save a bit more.

(c) we just can't afford it.

(d) we have decided to give some extra money to a Bible college being started in Indonesia this year.

Responses (a) and (b) we have all heard and can relate to. Response (c) we use all the time. But what of response (d)? From time to time we should inform our children that we have chosen to give our money away for the sake of the gospel. If we don't teach them this they will not know of the joy and obligation that there is in giving. They will not learn that choices are involved in how we use our money and they will think that the only limiting factor in spending is "we can't afford it". Let us not be ashamed of the gospel, not even in front of our children.

5. Get down to honest detail

Living as Christians in our money-centred society is not easy. After all, we cannot live totally independently of our society. Telephones, washing machines, computers, brick houses, cars, running shoes, pets, toys, books, good health ... we own and use all these things. Where is the line to be drawn between what is necessary to exist in our culture and what is chasing after Money?

I wish there were an easy answer. Ultimately, God alone knows the hearts of his people and we are called to give in secret, not demonstrating our generosity before men (Matt 6:1-4). Still, I offer a few practical proposals to fire our imaginations:

• Be content to be a few steps behind our peers in terms of our material possessions. One car instead of two. An old kitchen instead of a new one. A suit that dates from a few years ago. Instead of attending live concerts, buy the CD. Not updating the household computer for a couple of years. Postponing the piano class for the children. Of course, none of these actions might be appropriate for you. But the challenge is the same: contentment.

• Talk with your spouse and set a ceiling on how much your family budget will be, regardless of the salary. Set a 'lifestyle limit' and give the rest away. It is more and more common for both the wife and the husband to work. Sometimes it is a financial necessity. Sometimes it is because of the enjoyment that the employment offers. If the latter is the case, one salary could be given away entirely.

• Talk among ourselves at church, encouraging each other to be generous. Giving is done in secret, but encouragement to give can still be given. How easy it is for us to discuss the things we plan to buy or future investments. Instead, how can we turn conversations towards treasures in heaven and God's Kingdom?

• Consider, with excitement, what you can give to further God's Kingdom. Read. Pray. Find out more. Be imaginative. Churches needing resources in Kenya. A young evangelist needing training in Russia. Evangelistic missions in Cambodia. Theological training in Australia. Bibles to be distributed in Italy. Food for our brothers and sisters in Tanzania. Assisting our neighbour. Helping a widow in our church. Outreach to Muslims in the city suburbs. The family suffering from unemployment.

If you feel overwhelmed by the needs, that's appropriate! There is much to be done to proclaim Jesus' name in this world, and God has made us rich so that we can contribute generously. In 2 Corinthians 8, Paul cites a motivation for Christian giving that is rarely spoken of: equality within the household of God—and not simply within a congregation, but across congregations and across countries:

> I do not mean that others should be eased and you burdened, but that as a matter of fairness your abundance at the present time should supply their need, so that their abundance may supply your need, that there may be fairness. As it is written, "Whoever gathered much had nothing left over, and whoever gathered little had no lack" (2 Cor 8:13-15).

In various ways he wants to motivate their giving, and one such way is to remind them to show concern for those who are of God's household.

6. Make a concrete, immediate, radical change

In our materialistic society, it is difficult to know at what economic level to live. With whom do I compare myself? What are my expectations? What assets will help me better minister the gospel? What will I do without? How much can I give? What sacrifice will I make? Such choices are made on a day-to-day basis and, frankly, it can get pretty tiring to resist the pressures of our society to buy more and more and better and bigger. Everyone around us breathes such consumerism, even our Christian brothers and sisters. It is just exhausting to say 'no' continually or to have to stop and think about how to use money.

Why not take one step? Make one cutback, simple but radical. Make one choice that will mean that you step away from your peers. For example, skip the weekly family take-away meal. Drop the year's subscription to the theatre. Get rid of some of your investments. Put off the kids' private education—or scrap it altogether. Don't buy new clothes this year. Walk more and use the car less. Forget the overseas trip. Stop buying CDs for a year. Sell the holiday flat. Move into a smaller house.

Then—and here comes the exciting part—take out your cheque book and give away the money you have just saved.

There is no point in just becoming poorer. We do it for a reason—for the sake of the gospel. Cheerfully give away what you have so that God may use you as an instrument of his generosity. Such a lifestyle is radical. It is frightening, because we sense a loss of control over our lives. But it is, after all, in God alone that we put our confidence, and not Money. Furthermore, we are to follow the example of Jesus who "though he was rich, yet for your sakes he became poor, so that you through his poverty might become rich" (2 Cor 8:9). Now that we Christians are indeed thoroughly rich let us give away our fading riches so that those who are poor in this world may become rich in Christ.

VI

TRUE RICHES

CHAPTER 9

TRUE RICHES

THERE ARE MANY DIFFERENT sorts of rivalries in the various realms of human endeavour. Some engender mutual respect. This is true in many cases of sporting competition, whether the activity be athletics, chess, boxing or ice-skating. There have of course been famous exceptions where the opponents experienced little love for each other, and sometimes may even have wished their opponents ill (in ice-skating, Tonya Harding for Nancy Kerrigan, for instance; and in boxing, Mike Tyson for Evander Holyfield). Such animosity is more often the case in politics, and occurs almost without exception where two men are competing for the affections of the same woman. In such circumstances a better word to describe what the rivals feel for each other is 'contempt' rather than respect. And each is perhaps keener than ever to assert not just his own better qualities but his superiority to the other man on offer.

Oddly enough, as we saw in chapter 3, when God competes with money for our affection it is sometimes to amorous human relationships that he compares the rivalry. He experiences jealousy whenever human beings turn their back on him to worship idols. Riches threaten to replace God in the same way that the 'other man' is a threat to a marriage. Accordingly, in order to keep his bride, God not only runs down the opposition (stressing the futility and transience of riches) but also offers more than his rival. In other words, at the risk of sounding crass, if Mammon offers to make us rich, God promises to outbid him. The difference is that God's protestations of superiority over the other suitor, as so rarely in the human realm, are neither doubtful nor debatable. The riches God offers are in reality of far greater worth.

Better than gold

Just about everybody would like to get really rich. This is something that God realizes and uses to his advantage.

One of the substances most frequently mentioned in the Bible is gold. The supreme value, permanence and durability of gold are in no way disputed. Gold is associated with riches and power (Isa 60:17), characterized King Solomon's greatness (he "made silver and gold as common in Jerusalem as stone", 2 Chr 1:15), and was one of the three gifts presented to the infant Jesus by the wise men (Matt 2:11).

The marvel is that God offers something of even more value than gold. God's laws are more precious than gold (Ps 19:10). Wisdom from God is a better investment than gold (Prov 3:14, wisdom yields "profit better than gold"; also 8:10, 16:16). In fact, heaven itself is a city of pure gold (Rev 21:18, 21). Most importantly, in place of an excessive attachment to material wealth, God himself is to be our gold: "if you lay gold in the dust, and gold of Ophir among the stones of the torrent bed, then the Almighty will be your gold and your precious silver" (Job 22:24–25).

If the attraction of wealth is the prospect of enjoying an abundance of material goods, it is no accident that the Bible uses the language of abundance for spiritual goodness: God's abundant goodness (Pss 31:19, 145:7), mercy (Pss 51:1, 69:16), power (Ps 145:6–7), grace (Rom 5:17), salvation, wisdom and knowledge (Isa 33:6) bring to his people consolation (2 Cor 1:5), joy (2 Cor 8:2) and peace (2 Pet 1:2) in abundance.

The promise of true riches both now and in the age to come is also offered in the New Testament, and frequently in the context of, and as a comfort in, financial loss. There are many examples.

In Mark 10:29–30, Jesus promises that those who have left homes or fields for his sake will receive a hundred times as much in return to make up for their losses.

In 1 Corinthians 6:9–11, Paul encourages Christians to suffer being defrauded (6:7–8) with the promise of inheriting God's kingdom.

In 2 Corinthians 8:9, Paul reminds the Corinthians of their becoming rich through Christ's poverty in part to undergird his plea for their involvement in the collection for the poor in Jerusalem.

In Philippians 4:19, the Philippian Christians are promised blessing "according to [God's] riches in glory in Christ Jesus" in return for their financial contribution to Paul's support.

1 Timothy 6:5–6 turns the tables on the false teachers (who are looking to get rich through religion) by asserting that godliness with contentment brings great spiritual (rather than material) gain.

The rich in 1 Timothy 6:18–19 are to be "rich in good works" by giving generously, thereby laying up "treasure for themselves as a good foundation for the future".

In Hebrews 10:34, those who "joyfully accepted the plundering of [their] property" did so in the knowledge that they have "a better possession and an abiding one".

Paul described himself paradoxically as "having nothing, yet possessing everything" (2 Cor 6:10).

The most graphic example appears at the end of

Revelation, where the people of God who are told to 'come out' of doomed Babylon with all her riches (18:4) are given a vision of the new Jerusalem which more than compensates. If Babylon's wealth is to fall, the new Jerusalem's wealth is eternal and incorruptible, "having the glory of God, its radiance like a most rare jewel, like a jasper, clear as crystal" (21:11). The "fine linen" which clothed the "great city" in 18:16 is eclipsed by the "fine linen" which adorns the Lamb's bride in 19:8. The new Jerusalem's wealth far outweighs that which Revelation's readers are called to shun.

Thus young people who give up a lucrative career and the prospect of financial security to pursue aid work or full-time Christian service often see the matter in an entirely different light from those who look on and admire (or deride) their willingness to forgo riches. From their own point of view they have done nothing of the sort. When they sing the fourth verse of *Be Thou my vision, O Lord of my heart*,[1] a hymn which derives from an eighth-century Irish poem, they mean it:

> *Riches I heed not, nor man's empty praise,*
> *Thou mine inheritance now and always;*
> *Thou, and thou only, first in my heart,*
> *High King of heaven, my treasure thou art.*

Believers whose faith has somehow cost them materially are not thinking straight if they reckon they have missed out. Echoing the sentiments of Jesus, who said you'd be better off passing up the whole world if it meant forfeiting your soul (Matt 16:26), the missionary and martyr Jim Elliot once observed, "He is no fool who gives what he cannot keep to gain what he cannot lose". Similarly, the great nineteenth-century Baptist preacher Charles Haddon Spurgeon observed: "We need not covet money, for we shall always have our God, and God is better than gold, his favour is better than fortune".[2]

Finding treasure

Perhaps the most disturbing text on wealth in the entire Bible is Revelation 3:17–18, where some who say, "I am rich, I have prospered, and I need nothing" (the unwritten slogan of many a well-to-do suburb), are described as "wretched, pitiable, poor, blind and naked". They are told to "buy ... gold refined by fire, so that you may be rich" in order to remedy the situation. But surely this advice is preposterous at best, and at worst cruel and perverse. How can those described as 'poor' ever hope to afford fine gold? You may as well tell a blind person to read print, or an infant to run a marathon. This is of course to read the verses in a naïvely literalistic fashion. The non-literal use of the notion of riches is well known. Outside of the religious sphere, people sometimes talk of having their lives *enriched* by grandchildren, music or a garden, none of which has anything to do with money. And social commentators have always distinguished between 'standard of living' (a purely economic measure) and 'quality of life'.

The figurative use of the notions of poverty and riches in Revelation 3 is clearly meant to signify two things. First, those who are materially rich may not be really rich. Secondly, and even more alarmingly, spiritual riches are by no means within their budget. It recalls Isaiah's engaging invitation to "Come ... he who has no money ... Come, buy ... without money and without price" (55:1).

The command to buy fine gold, like the surprising description of the rich as actually being poor, is deliberately worded to give those who are smug and self-satisfied, those who think they are doing rather well thank you very much, pause for thought. Verses 19–20 of Revelation 3 give some indication as to what is meant, using the old-fashioned word "repent". If we are rich and want to get really rich, we are to start by admitting our spiritual bankruptcy, turn from our proud self-sufficiency and accept Jesus' offer of a personal relationship and friendship ("Behold, I stand at the door and knock", verse 20). In other words, we must seek God, in the firm knowledge that we will find him only because in the first place he is seeking us.

The Christian gospel of acceptance with God, not on the basis of what we do but on what he has done (in sending his Son to secure our release from the power and penalty of sin), uses a variety of expressions to instruct us how we ought to respond. The most familiar are faith (towards God) and repentance (from sin). The same action, however, can be characterized as receiving (Christ), obeying (his authoritative summons), hearing (his call), and, more metaphorically, as waking up (from a deep sleep), drinking (his Spirit), eating (Christ's flesh) and buying (his gold). They all mean basically the same thing. The last expression is particularly apt for those who consider themselves to be rich, for it simultaneously registers with them (they are used to such transactions) and horrifies them (they can't afford it).

If buying fine gold (in this letter to the church in Laodicea) signifies the way of entry into a personal relationship with God, two other purchases (verse 18) indicate what will result from this act of repentance.

First, the Laodiceans' shameful nakedness would be remedied by buying "white garments to wear". Nakedness is a biblical symbol for humiliation on the day of judgment, fine clothes for honour and forgiveness. In Revelation, white clothes in particular are worn by those who live in the presence of God (cf. 3:4–5; 4:4; 7:9; 19:14). Revelation 7:14 explains that such robes have been washed in the blood of the Lamb. The harshness of the condemnation of the rich in this passage is more than matched by the magnanimous offer of mercy and restoration. It is out of love that the rebuke is offered in the first place (3:19). Once we arrive at the point of admitting the folly of the sin of greed, there is available to us full pardon and complete forgiveness on the basis of Christ's sacrificial death. It is simply a matter of getting dressed.

One of the biggest obstacles for many people in relation to this much-misunderstood business of repentance towards God is that it all sounds too good to be true. Often the problem is not unbelief so much as disbelief. The truth is, however, that what so many of us crave is exactly what is on offer, namely a fresh start. When Zacchaeus, the greedy tax collector, came to Jesus (Luke 19:1–10), it was the crowd, not Jesus, who regarded him as literally beyond redemption. Jesus took the initiative and invited himself into Zacchaeus' house. Zacchaeus' decision to open the door led to Jesus' startling affirmation that 'Today salvation has come to this house' and to his own radical about-turn: "Behold, Lord, the half of my goods I give to the poor. And if I have defrauded anyone of anything, I restore it fourfold".

Secondly, the Laodiceans' blindness would be remedied by buying "salve" to put on their eyes, so they could see. As we noted earlier, greed is basically a problem of vision. What you see is what you get, or at least what you try to get. Those who repent are promised not only forgiveness but also transformation, resulting from authentic healing. They have the opportunity to stop behaving like everyone else in town and act out a new set of priorities and values. In short, they will see things differently and act accordingly, or see something better than material things and go after it.

Strictly speaking, the Bible's solution to greed is not to stop wanting to be rich. To expect that of human beings would be unrealistic. There is no point just telling people to stop seeking and running after riches. Such desires need to be not quashed so much as redirected. In Colossians 3, believers are not only to put to death earthly greed, which is idolatry (3:5), but also and instead to set their minds on things above, not on earthly things (3:1–2). Likewise, in the context of Jesus' saying that you cannot serve God and money/Mammon, the teaching against greed is introduced with the injunction to lay up treasures not on earth but in heaven (Matt 6:19), and closes with the call to seek first God's kingdom and righteousness (verse 33) instead of the material things which the Gentiles seek (verse 32). In 1 Timothy 6:10–11 it is not enough just to run away from greed; the godly person is also to run after something: the way to flee the love of money is to pursue God and godly virtues.

The importance of replacing evil desires with holy ones was seen by the Church Father Augustine, who wrote, "Let not these occupy my soul; rather let God occupy it".[3] True riches consist of having a stake in the life of the true and living God. To recall the two texts upon which the reflections of this book have been based, if greed is idolatry (Col 3:5), and you are disinclined to place too much stock on material things, then it is worth remembering that "there is great gain in godliness with contentment" (1 Tim 6:6).

If the greedy find pleasure and fulfilment in their possessions, in God's presence we are filled with joy and at his right hand are eternal pleasures (Ps 16:11). The task and privilege of the Christian is to glorify God, but also to enjoy him. Human beings are incomplete and ultimately dissatisfied until they are right with God, who, at great cost—not that of silver and gold, but of the blood of his dear Son—has purchased our redemption. What we see around us is not all there is and ever will be. We can fight God, or ignore him, or replace him with any manner of substitutes, including material wealth; but to do any of these is futile and a folly and can only lead to disappointment.

If the greedy look to their riches for confidence and security, God offers a far superior and harder currency, one which has no risk of exposure to instability or devaluation. The person who is really rich has come to a settled confidence and trust in God, who made the world and everything in it. Such a person affirms that "There is none like God ... The eternal God is [my] dwelling place, and underneath are the everlasting arms" (Deut 33:26–27). Even if an economic (or natural) disaster comes upon them, they affirm with Paul that nothing "will be able to separate us from the love of God in Christ Jesus" (Rom 8:35–39).

If the greedy eventually find themselves in a demeaning and destructive slavery to Mammon, resenting their bondage, the person who is really rich has discovered true liberty and freedom in serving God, who himself took the form of a servant in Christ. The train is truly free only when it runs on the tracks, and, however inviting the alternative might appear, it would come to a grinding halt if it were free to plough into the field. "If the Son sets you free, you will be free indeed" (John 8:36).

Having your cake

But does it have to be 'either/or'? Can't a person be both materially rich and rich towards God at the same time? Why not aim at both sorts of riches? The Bible doesn't, in fact, rule out the possibility; calls to voluntary poverty are fairly rare, and the rich are not always told to give it all away. But neither does the Bible encourage such thinking; it is never shy of questioning our motives and underscoring our proneness to self-deception. Seeking God is meant to be a lifelong, all-consuming, all-embracing passion, which does not so much rule out the goal of getting rich as squeeze it out.

The Jewish philosopher Philo of Alexandria, who was a contemporary of Paul, asked with great insight, "of what riches can we any longer stand in need, when we have you, who alone is true riches?"[4] In the final analysis it is a matter of priorities. Which do you crave more, to be rich, or to be really rich?

Desire not only orders our lives, it also informs our prayers. Proverbs 30:8–9 contains a prayer which strikes the right balance:

Remove far from me falsehood and lying;
give me neither poverty nor riches;
feed me with the food that is needful for me,
lest I be full and deny you
and say, "Who is the LORD?"
or lest I be poor and steal
and profane the name of my God.

The danger that wealth will lead to pride and blasphemy means that for most of us it is simply better not to get rich. The pitfalls of both poverty and wealth seem so inevitable that the prayer asks (literally) for 'food of my portion', no more and no less—a modest sufficiency. Wealth often leads to feeling we have no need of God and ultimately to denying him. It is better to be denied wealth than to have wealth and to deny God.

Get a life

*For what will it profit a man if he gains the whole
world and forfeits his life?* (MATT 16:26).

As put-downs go, 'Get a life' is steeply condescending and
devastatingly comprehensive. It may be turned on its head,
however, and said to those who mistakenly think that life is
about material possessions, and that life consists of food and
the body of clothing (cf. Matt 6:25b).

'Get a life' in fact summarizes the Bible's ultimate diagnosis of what's wrong with greed, and prescribes its most
effective cure. Jesus summed up his mission in terms of
bringing life in its abundance (John 10:10). Deuteronomy
30:19 calls us to "choose life", not as a nasty taunt, but as a
winsome invitation. And 1 Timothy 6, which offers a warn-
ing against the love of money, concludes by exhorting its
readers to "take hold of that which is truly life" (verse 19b).

*Now there is great gain in godliness with contentment,
for we brought nothing into the world, and we cannot
take anything out of the world. But if we have food
and clothing, with these we will be content. But those
who desire to be rich fall into temptation, into a snare,
into many senseless and harmful desires that plunge
people into ruin and destruction. For the love of money
is a root of all kinds of evils. It is through this craving
that some have wandered away from the faith and
pierced themselves with many pangs.*

*But as for you, O man of God, flee these things. Pursue
righteousness, godliness, faith, love, steadfastness,
gentleness. Fight the good fight of the faith. Take hold of
the eternal life to which you were called ...*

As for the rich in this present age, charge them not to be haughty, nor to set their hopes on the uncertainty of riches, but on God, who richly provides us with everything to enjoy. They are to do good, to be rich in good works, to be generous and ready to share, thus storing up treasure for themselves as a good foundation for the future, so that they may take hold of that which is truly life (1 TIM 6:6–12A, 17–19).

ENDNOTES

1. This hymn was translated from the original Gaelic into English in 1905 by Mary Byrne (1880–1931) and later versified by Eleanor Hull (1860–1935).
2. Cited in John Blanchard (ed.), *More Gathered Gold: A Treasury of Quotations for Christians* (Welwyn: Evangelical Press, 1986), p. 64.
3. Augustine, *Confessions* 10.51.
4. Philo, *On Dreams* 1.179.

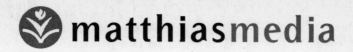
matthiasmedia

Matthias Media is an independent, evangelical, non-denominational company based in Sydney, Australia. We produce an extensive range of Bible studies, books, Bible reading materials, evangelistic tools, training resources, periodicals and multimedia resources. In all that we do, our mission is:

To serve our Lord Jesus Christ, and the growth of his gospel in Australia and the world, by producing and delivering high quality, Bible-based resources.

For more information about our resources, and to browse our online catalogue, visit our website at **www.matthiasmedia.com.au**. (US customers may visit: www.matthiasmedia.com. In the UK and Europe, our resources are distributed by The Good Book Company at www.thegoodbook.co.uk.)

You can also contact us in any of the following ways:

Mail:	Matthias Media PO Box 225 Kingsford NSW 2032 Australia
Telephone:	1800 814 360 *(tollfree in Australia)* 9663 1478 *(in Sydney)* +61 2 9663 1478 *(international)*
Facsimile:	9663 3265 *(in Sydney)* +61 2 9663 3265 *(international)*
Email:	info@matthiasmedia.com.au

Other Resources from Matthias Media